Paper Masks and Puppets

Paper Masks and Puppets

for Stories, Songs and Plays

 The Arts Factory
Seattle, Washington

Written by
Ron and Marsha Feller

Photographs by
Hermon Joyner

Designed and
Illustrated by
Kathryn Kusché Hastings

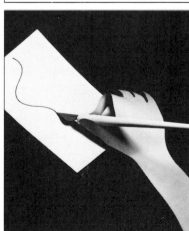

Second printing, 1986

Grateful acknowledgment is made to
Dover Publications, Inc., New York, for
the paper bird mask from the book *Com-
plete Book of Paper Mask Making* by
Michael Grater, copyright © 1967 by
Michael Grater, Dover edition first pub-
lished in 1984. Reprinted by permission of
Dover Publications, Inc., and Michael Grater.

**Library of Congress Cataloging-in-
Publication Data**

Feller, Ron, 1942-
   Paper masks and puppets for stories,
songs, and plays.

   1. Paper work.   2. Masks.   3. Puppets
and puppet-plays in education.   4. Drama
in education.   I. Feller, Marsha, 1944-   .
II. Joyner, Hermon.   III. Hastings,
Kathryn Kusché.   IV. Title.
TT870.F45   1985   745.54   85-72952
ISBN 0-9615873-0-X (pbk.)

Publication of this book was made possible
in part by the Washington Alliance for Arts
Education, a component of the Education
Program of the John F. Kennedy Center for
the Performing Arts, Washington, D.C.

/AF The Arts Factory
     P.O. Box 55547
     Seattle, WA 98155

Printed in the United States of America

First Edition

To all the kids, parents, teachers and friends who gave us so much
encouragement and support, we dedicate this book.

Foreword

The Washington Alliance for Arts Education is part of a nationwide network of professional organizations that share in a commitment to promote arts education and quality arts experiences. We believe that Ron and Marsha Feller in their work with children and educators provide valid and exciting avenues for learning.

Ron and Marsha have been professional storytellers since 1974 and have performed in schools throughout the country. They have taught workshops for educators in most of our nation's major cities and have been eager instructors at young writers' conferences, Very Special Arts Festivals and Cultural Enrichment Programs.

This book reflects the many talents of these two exceptional art educators. With Ron's keen knowledge of art and music, and Marsha's background in dance and drama, you, the reader, will be introduced to a myriad of ways to glorify reading, creative writing and leisure play.

The Washington Alliance for Arts Education is pleased to be affiliated with the creation of this book. We find it a genuine reflection of Ron and Marsha's delightful energy and their enthusiasm for the arts process.
— Jan Graves, Vice Chair, Publications, W.A.A.E.

Acknowledgments

We would like to give special thanks to:

Jan Graves and the Washington Alliance for Arts Education for initiating this project; Phyllis Luvera Ennes for her hours of editing and her continued encouragement; Michael Grater, master paper artist, for spending time with us and exchanging paper working ideas.

We would also like to thank all those who have given special support to our work over the years:

Mickie Clise, Jeanne Crawford, Myrtle Dahlin, Carolyn Eddington, Gene Fink, Ernie Forge, Cathy Hardison, Ken Kraintz, Ralph Larsen, Nick Mason, Cathy Mears, Muriel Miller, Susan Pearson, Randy Rockhill, and the Washington State Arts Commission.

Finally, we would like to thank the wonderful boys and girls who appear in the photographs in this book:

Paul Crooks, Kathy and Michael Pottratz, Amy and Tony Ressa, Heidi and Max von Marbod, Kelly and Benji Ward.

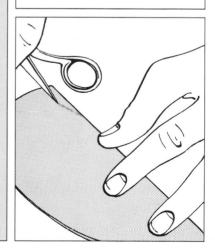

Contents

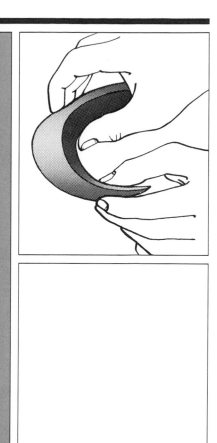

Introduction

Kids say . . .   "Will you teach me how to make a mask?"

Parents say . . .   "Don't you have a book showing all those projects? I'd love to do more with my kids at home."

"Do you have anything I can show my husband for his Boy Scout troop?"

"Our church group would love to do these activities. Do you have anything I can share with them?"

Teachers say . . .   "I wish I'd brought my camera so I can remember all those examples. Don't you have a handout or something I can take back to my class to use for reference?"

Well, after eleven years of saying, "We'll have to write a book someday," we can finally say, "Yes!" to all these questions.

Paper Masks and Puppets for Stories, Songs and Plays is a book describing the process we use to help kids and adults feel more comfortable with the arts.

The first part of the book is a detailed description on how to make masks and puppets out of paper and other simple materials that are readily available.

The second part of the book shows how the masks and puppets can be used to help create stories, songs and plays.

These projects can be used in many ways:
- ☐ Teachers can integrate them into their curriculum . . . music, drama and art activities make lessons come to life and reach a deeper, unmeasurable level in the students. Writing motivation is "built-in."
- ☐ Parents can work with their children on these projects at home. It's a good way to strengthen family ties and closer parent-child relationships.
- ☐ Kids can do these projects with other kids or on their own. The directions and diagrams are done with them in mind.

The main thing to remember is that these projects need to be **USED**. They want to leap out from the pages of this book and come to life. With your help, they will.

Some people will jump in; others will *e-a-s-e* in . . . No matter what . . .

DON'T HESITATE . . . PARTICIPATE!

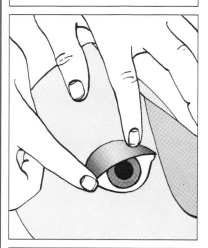

Materials

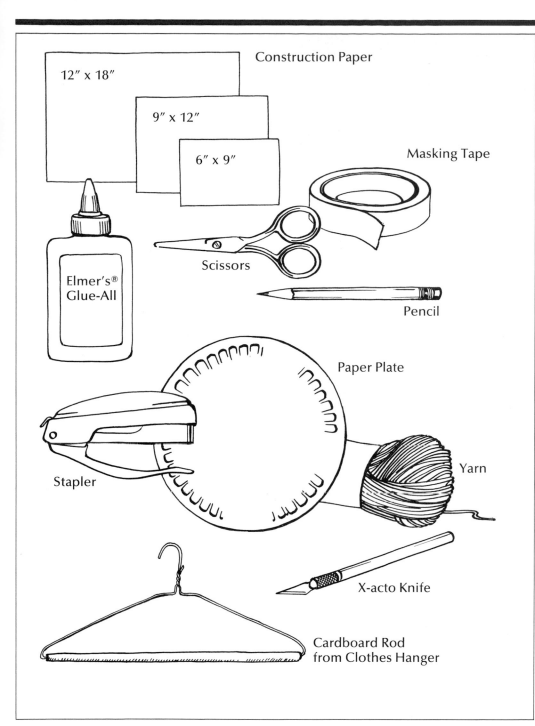

Construction Paper

12" x 18"

9" x 12"

6" x 9"

Masking Tape

Elmer's® Glue-All

Scissors

Pencil

Paper Plate

Stapler

Yarn

X-acto Knife

Cardboard Rod from Clothes Hanger

Most of the masks and puppets in this book can be made easily with the materials shown on this page.

Construction paper, 12" x 18" and 9" x 12", is recommended for most of the projects. Decorating pieces can be cut down to 6" x 9" rectangles, or scraps can be used. Strathmore 300 Colored Art Paper, however, produces a more durable mask. (All of the masks photographed for this book were made from Strathmore paper.)

Elmer's Glue-All has a consistency thick enough to glue scored pieces without having to use tabs.

A hand-held stapler is easy to control, and there is less chance of damaging the paper.

Lightweight, inexpensive paper plates, 9" in diameter, work well as backing for the hand-held masks.

Cardboard rods from clothes hangers are used for the hand-held puppets and marionettes, though a tightly rolled sheet of 12" x 18" construction paper will substitute if the rods are not available.

X-acto knives will come in handy, but they are not essential.

Paper Working Techniques

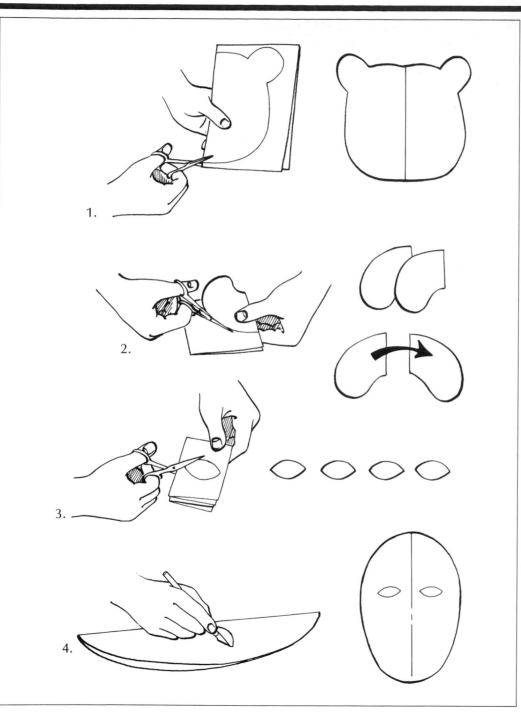

FOLDING TO CREATE SYMMETRICAL SHAPES

A method used repeatedly in this book is to fold a piece of paper before cutting to create a symmetrical shape.

1. A shape drawn and cut from the folded edge will create one symmetrical shape.

2. A shape drawn and cut from the non-folded edges will create two identical shapes.

3. If several identical shapes are desired, cut them at the same time. (Use scraps whenever possible.)

4. If identical holes or slits are needed on a mask, refold the mask before cutting to make sure the holes or slits are symmetrically placed. An X-acto knife is recommended for this task.

SCORING

Scoring is a way of giving a flat piece of paper three-dimensional qualities. This is done by drawing the point of the scissors across the paper. The line that is made should break the fiber but not go through the paper.

Fold paper in half before scoring if two identical scored shapes are needed.

Practice this paper shaping technique on scrap paper so you will know how hard to press with the scissors.

Try curved lines, straight lines . . . there are endless possibilities.

1. Pull the scissors toward you.

2. Cut out the desired shape.

3. Bend along the scored line.

OR . . .

Cut out the shape first, then score.

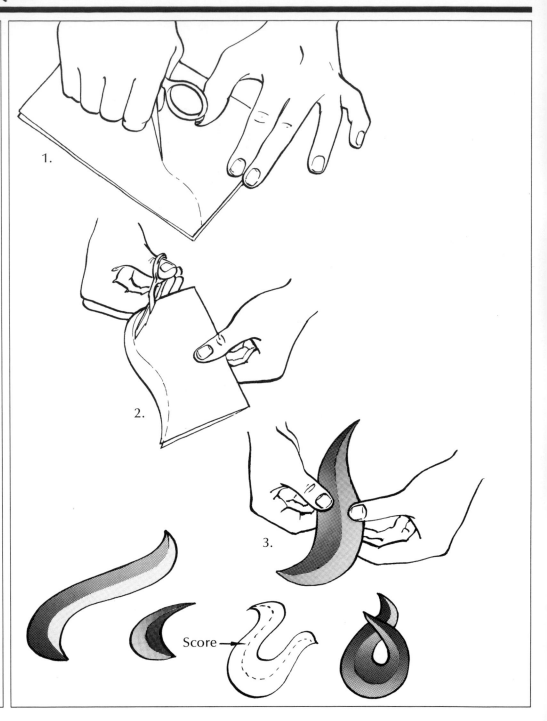

Score →

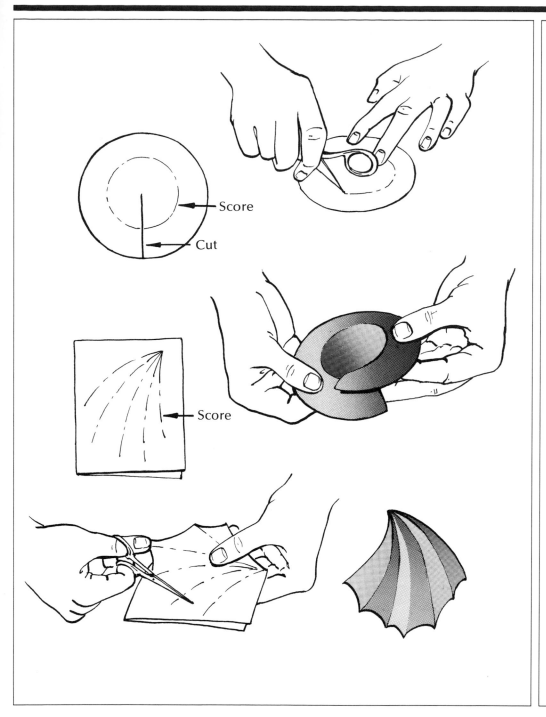

Score

Cut

Score

Score

To make circular folds, cut out a circle and score a smaller circle within.

Make a cut to the center of the circle.

Overlap the cut edges while gently bending the scored lines.

Secure with glue.

When multiple lines are scored, they are bent in opposite directions. These multiple lines can be straight, curved or circular.

Remember: You can cut out a shape and then score down the middle . . .

OR . . .

as illustrated, score first and then cut out shape around the scored line.

CUTTING DESIGNS

Another way of adding texture and design to a flat piece of paper is to cut shapes with an X-acto knife and bend them outward.

1. Trace the shapes to create a pattern using a paper template.

2. Cut out all but one edge of the shape using an X-acto knife. (Be sure to use cardboard or a cutting mat underneath.)

3. Score at the base.

4. Fold outward.

Note: To make a pattern of equal spaces, draw a grid on the back to use as a guide for placement of the template.

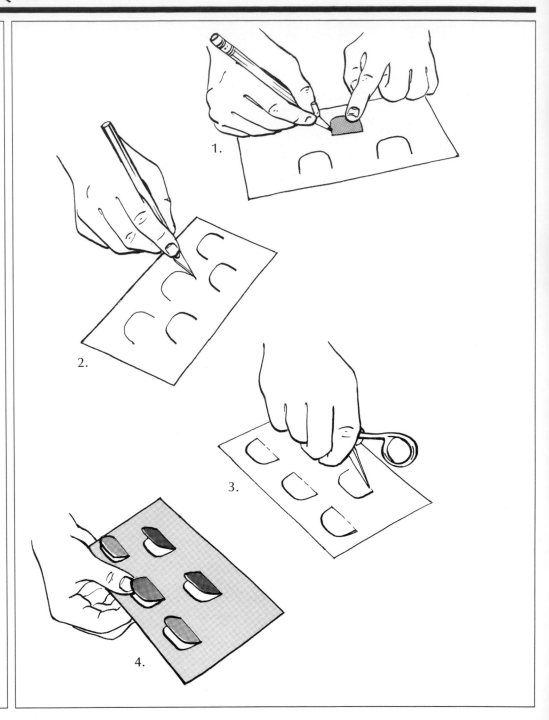

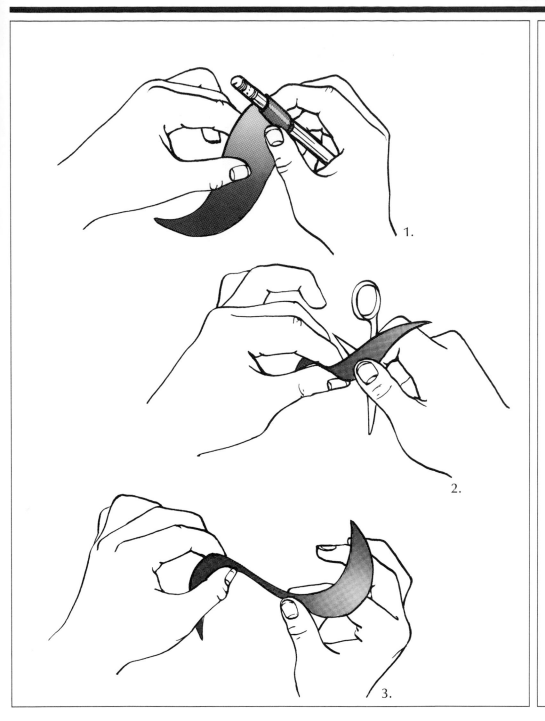

CURLING

Curling paper is another way to add three-dimensional shapes to a mask or puppet. Try some of these methods.

1. Wrap paper around a pencil and gently remove the pencil.

2. Pull paper across a scissors blade as you would with ribbon.

3. Pull paper gently between tip of thumb and index finger.

MAKING FRINGES, SPIRALS AND SPRINGS

Fringes, spirals and springs can add interesting movement to masks and puppets.

1. Make a series of parallel cuts along a strip to create a fringe. Cut twice as many by folding the paper in half before cutting. Roll the base of the fringe to make an interesting topknot. Try curling the strands of the fringe around a pencil. Mix sizes and colors of fringes together for varied effects.

2. Cut a spiral from a circular piece of paper to add interesting dimension.

3. Make a spring by gluing two strips of paper at right angles and folding the strip on the bottom over the top. Continue folding in this fashion. Use these springs to lift features off the surface of masks.

MAKING A PAPER ROD

If a cardboard rod from a clothes hanger is not available, make one by tightly rolling a 12" x 18" sheet of construction paper. Roll diagonally and secure with tape.

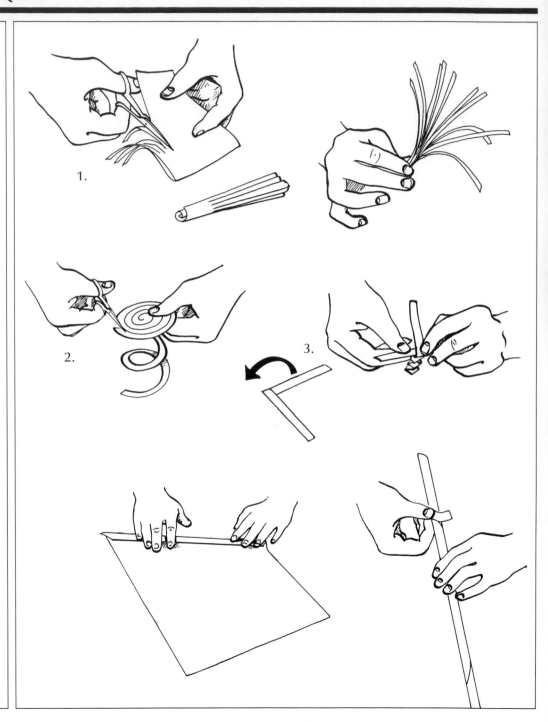

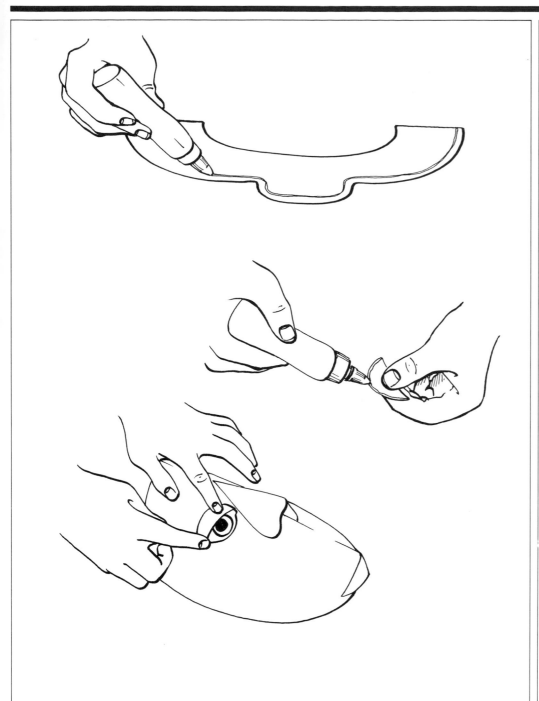

GLUING

Use glue sparingly . . . a little goes a long way.

Use the glue tip like a pencil. Touch the glue tip to the paper when applying glue, and use the tip to "draw" quickly around the edge of the shape.

Run a small bead of glue along the edge that is to be secured. (Most of the time, tabs are unnecessary.)

When gluing a scored piece to a surface, put spots of glue only on the places that touch the surface. Set the shape in position, and hold for a few seconds.

Caution: Be careful to keep the dimensional quality of the scored shape by not pressing down too hard in the gluing process.

Paper Masks and Puppets

Hand-Held Masks: Human Faces

MATERIALS

For one mask . . .

Construction paper
- At least one sheet, 12″ x 18″
- Several sheets of 6″ x 9″ paper in a variety of colors for features

Elmer's Glue-All

Pencil

Scissors

Hand-Held Stapler

A White Paper Plate, 9″ in diameter

A Cardboard Rod from a Clothes Hanger

Masking Tape

Optional:
X-acto Knife

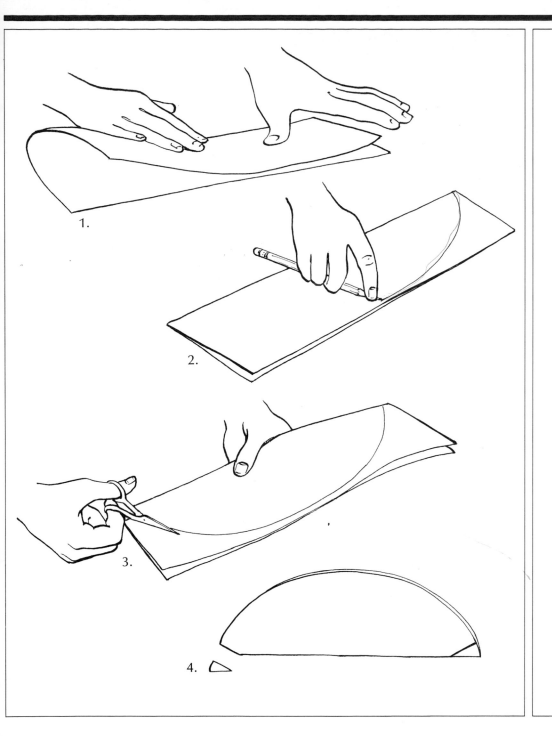

BASIC HEAD SHAPE

1. Fold a piece of 12" x 18" construction paper in half, lengthwise.

2. Draw half an oval in this space from the folded side. Be sure to fill up most of this space.

3. Cut out the shape.

4. Cut out small "pie shapes" at either end.

5. Bring the paper together, overlapping at the "pie shapes," and staple. This forms the chin and the top of the head.

6. Staple a paper plate to the back of the mask as shown. The "eating side" of the paper plate should be facing outward. If some of the paper plate shows from the front, trim it away. (Attaching the paper plate adds strength to the mask and provides a base for securing the clothes hanger rod.)

Alternative:

Another way to form a chin is to score the "pie shape" instead of cutting it out.

Folding the scored lines as shown creates a valley fold which makes a chin indentation.

Attach to a paper plate.

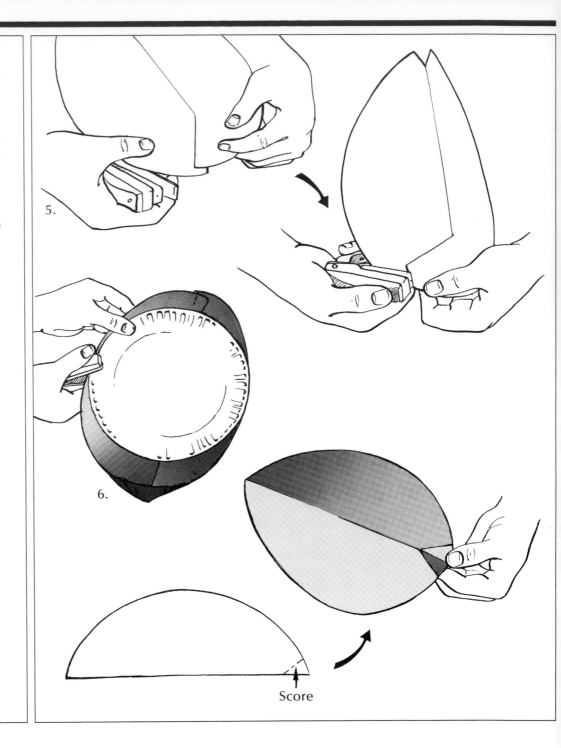

5.

6.

Score

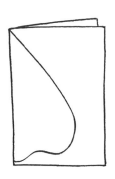

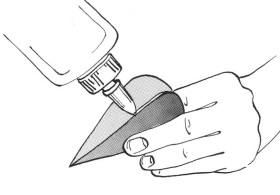

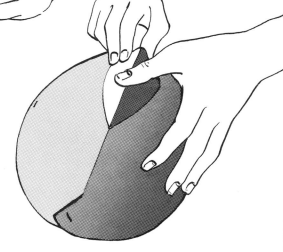

NOSES

Fold a rectangular piece of paper (approximately 6" x 9") in half, either lengthwise or widthwise.

Cut one half a nose shape from the folded edge. Draw it first if necessary.

Noses can be different sizes and shapes but are basically triangular.

Crease the bridge of the nose well. Run glue along the edges of the nose as shown. Be careful not to flatten the nose when attaching.

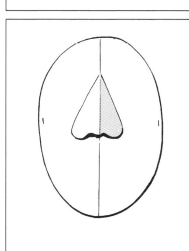

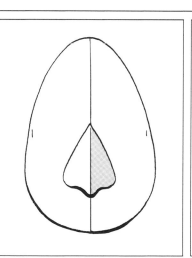

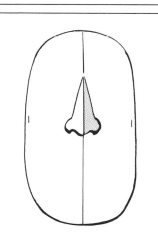

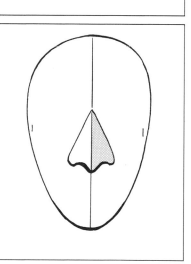

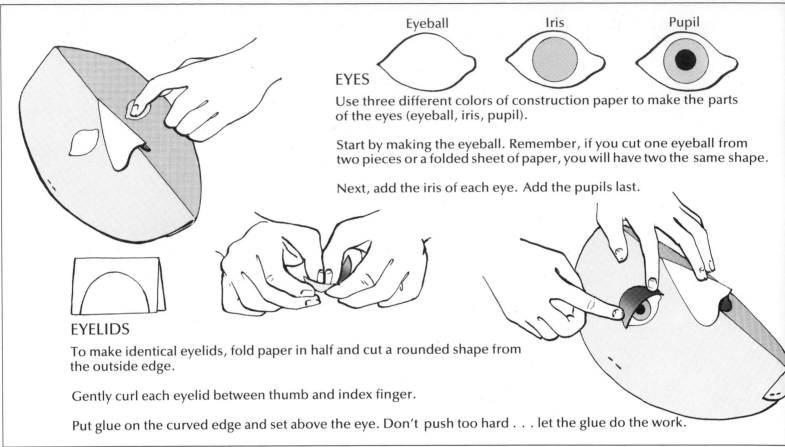

Eyeball   Iris   Pupil

EYES

Use three different colors of construction paper to make the parts of the eyes (eyeball, iris, pupil).

Start by making the eyeball. Remember, if you cut one eyeball from two pieces or a folded sheet of paper, you will have two the same shape.

Next, add the iris of each eye. Add the pupils last.

EYELIDS

To make identical eyelids, fold paper in half and cut a rounded shape from the outside edge.

Gently curl each eyelid between thumb and index finger.

Put glue on the curved edge and set above the eye. Don't push too hard . . . let the glue do the work.

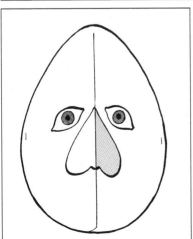
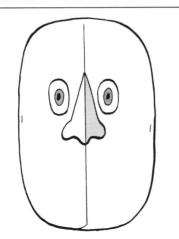
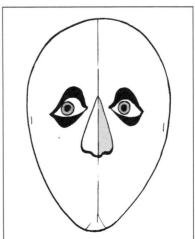
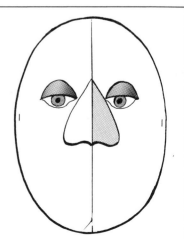

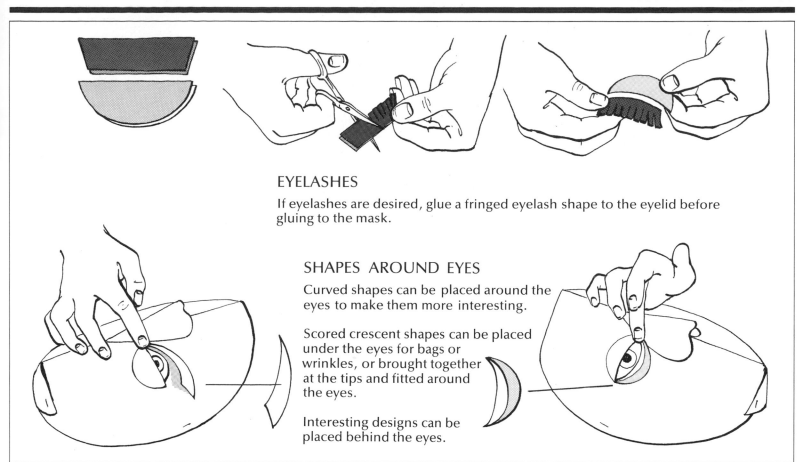

EYELASHES

If eyelashes are desired, glue a fringed eyelash shape to the eyelid before gluing to the mask.

SHAPES AROUND EYES

Curved shapes can be placed around the eyes to make them more interesting.

Scored crescent shapes can be placed under the eyes for bags or wrinkles, or brought together at the tips and fitted around the eyes.

Interesting designs can be placed behind the eyes.

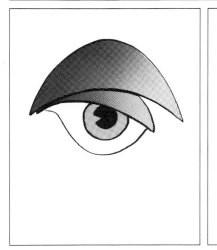

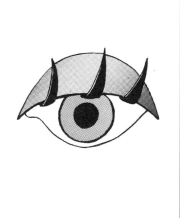

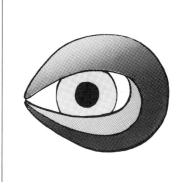

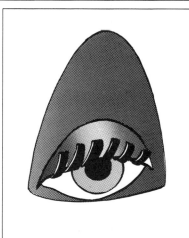

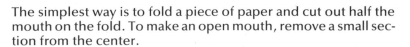

MOUTHS

There are several ways to make mouths.

The simplest way is to fold a piece of paper and cut out half the mouth on the fold. To make an open mouth, remove a small section from the center.

The mouth does not have to be glued down flat. To give a raised effect to the lips, spot glue at the corners. Position mouth slightly lifted from the basic head shape. Hold until glue sets.

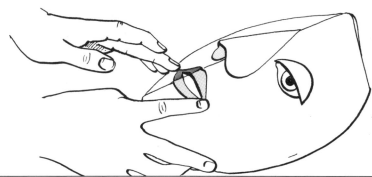

EYEBROWS

Cut two identical eyebrows from a folded sheet of paper.

Try fringing, scoring or curling for added interest.

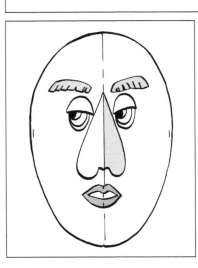

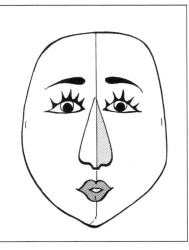

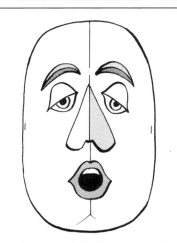

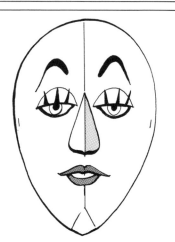

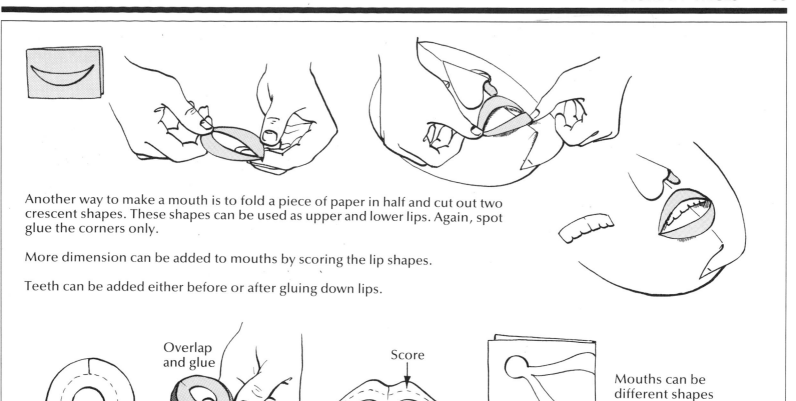

Another way to make a mouth is to fold a piece of paper in half and cut out two crescent shapes. These shapes can be used as upper and lower lips. Again, spot glue the corners only.

More dimension can be added to mouths by scoring the lip shapes.

Teeth can be added either before or after gluing down lips.

Mouths can be different shapes and sizes depending on the character being made.

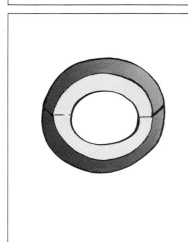

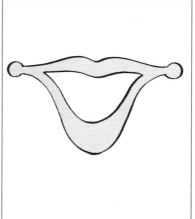

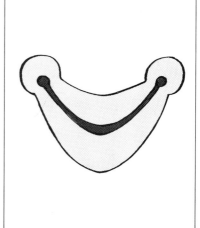

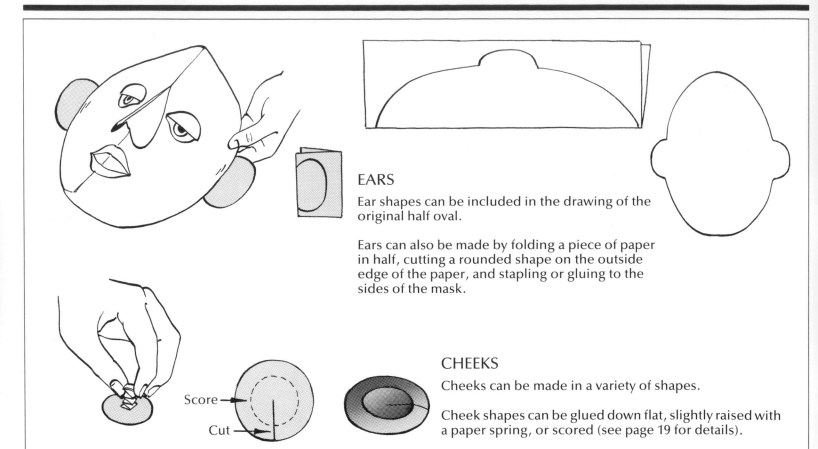

EARS

Ear shapes can be included in the drawing of the original half oval.

Ears can also be made by folding a piece of paper in half, cutting a rounded shape on the outside edge of the paper, and stapling or gluing to the sides of the mask.

Score

Cut

CHEEKS

Cheeks can be made in a variety of shapes.

Cheek shapes can be glued down flat, slightly raised with a paper spring, or scored (see page 19 for details).

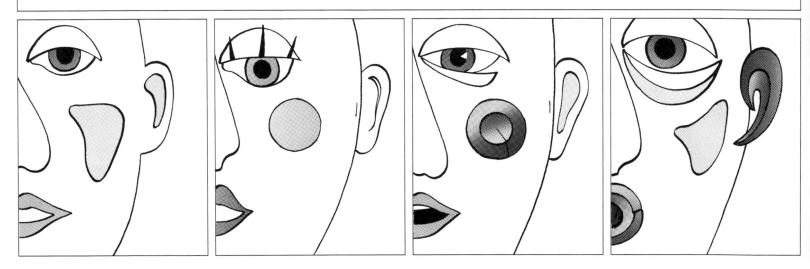

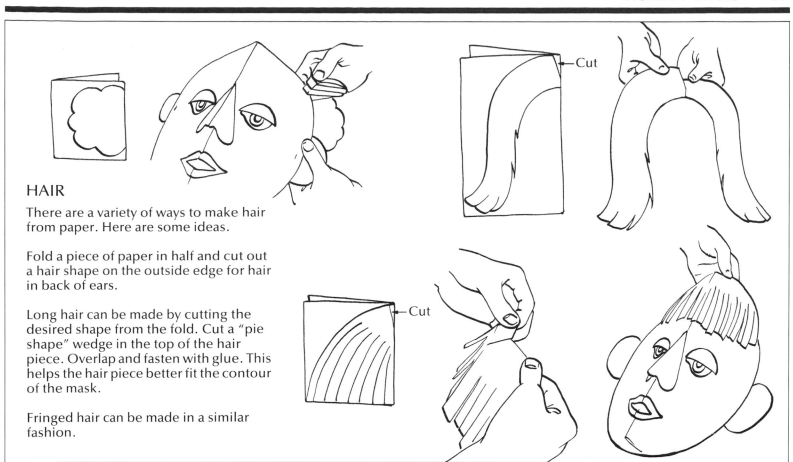

HAIR

There are a variety of ways to make hair from paper. Here are some ideas.

Fold a piece of paper in half and cut out a hair shape on the outside edge for hair in back of ears.

Long hair can be made by cutting the desired shape from the fold. Cut a "pie shape" wedge in the top of the hair piece. Overlap and fasten with glue. This helps the hair piece better fit the contour of the mask.

Fringed hair can be made in a similar fashion.

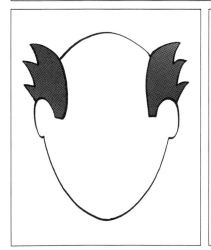

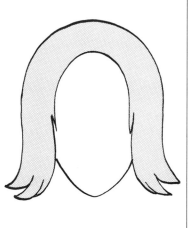

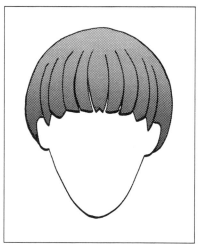

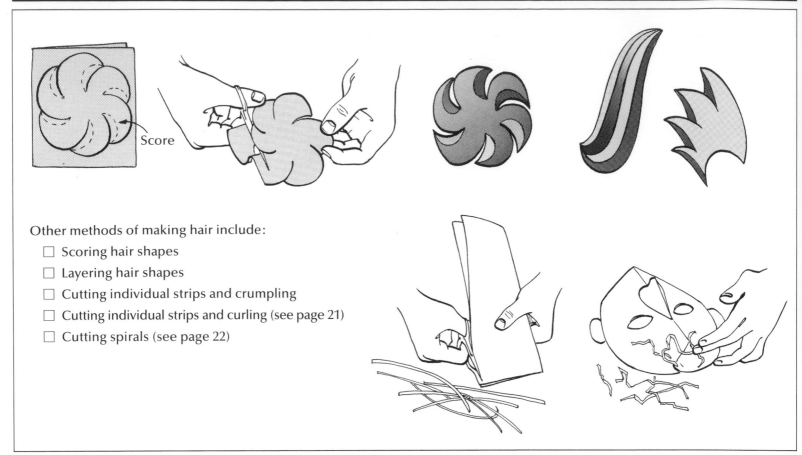

Other methods of making hair include:

☐ Scoring hair shapes

☐ Layering hair shapes

☐ Cutting individual strips and crumpling

☐ Cutting individual strips and curling (see page 21)

☐ Cutting spirals (see page 22)

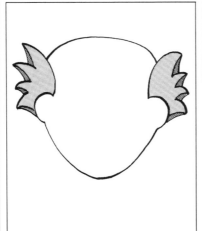

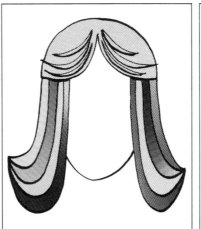

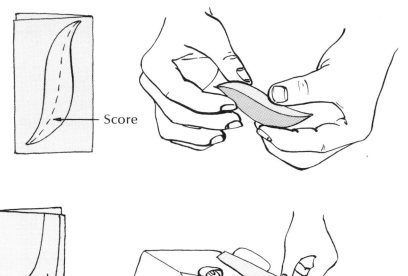

Score

MUSTACHES

The easiest way to make a mustache is to cut out half a mustache from the fold.

Another way is to cut two identical shapes and glue them symmetrically to the face shape.

Mustaches can be scored, fringed or curled.

BEARDS

As with mustaches, possibilities for shapes and sizes are endless: goatees, short or long beards, layered beards, beards with sideburns . . .

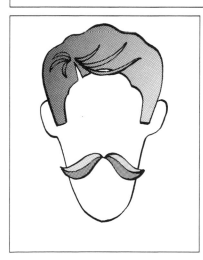

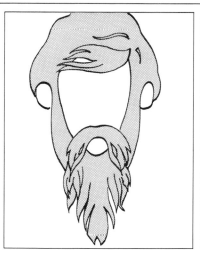

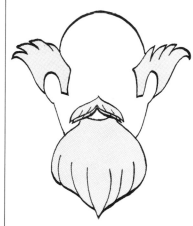

HATS, CROWNS AND BOWS

Dress up your mask with hats, crowns, bow ties, ruffles, flowers . . .

Tab for gluing.

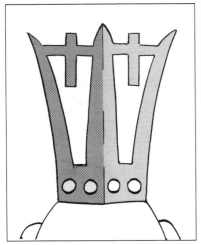

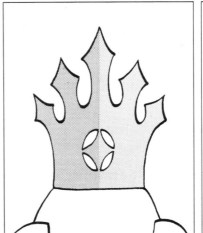

Score

CLOWNS AND JESTERS

Try some of the following ideas for clowns and jesters.

Try a two-piece face. Glue a large mouth unit on an "upper" head piece.

Add a ruffle. Cut and score.

For a dramatic background shape behind the eyes:

1.
Cut out the background shape first.

2.
Trace the shape on a darker color to create the eyebrows.

3.
Trace and cut out the eyebrows.

4.
Glue the eyebrows to the first shape.

5.
Add the eyeball-iris-pupil combination.

6.
Add eyelids if desired.

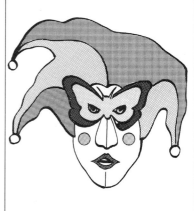

FANCIFUL CHARACTERS

When making trolls, monsters and other "critters," it is not necessary to begin with an oval shape. Substitute an unusual, outrageous, free-form shape for the oval.

(In order to retain interesting lines in the chin and forehead, the "pie shape" cuts can be omitted.)

Exaggerate the features. Use bold colors and interesting shapes to decorate the mask. Experiment with three-dimensional shapes.

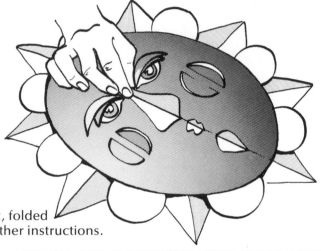

SUNS

To make a sun mask, start by drawing half a circle on a folded piece of paper.

After the face has been created, embellish by adding interesting shapes (geometric and/or free-form) in a pattern around the edge of the circle.

Note the use of cut and lifted features in the sun illustration on the right. The cheeks, nose, lips and chin are scored, cut, folded and lifted to create a dimensional effect. See page 20 for further instructions.

ATTACHING THE ROD

To complete the hand-held mask, attach a clothes hanger rod, a 12" stick or a piece of tightly rolled paper to the back of the paper plate with masking tape. Be sure the tape is "snugged up" to the rod before securing it to the paper plate.

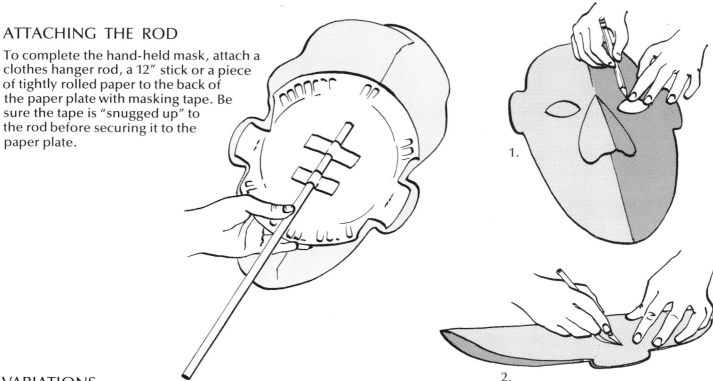

1.

2.

VARIATIONS

If the mask is to be worn, cut the oval as in the hand-held mask, but do not attach to a paper plate.

Cutting out the eyeholes is the traditional way to allow the wearer to see through the mask. A more unusual way, however, is to cut slits *under* the eyes.

1. Cut out a nose and two eye shapes and place in position on the mask. (Do not glue in place.) Trace around one eye. Set aside the nose and eye shapes.

2. Refold the mask. Draw a crescent shape under one eye, and cut it out with an X-acto knife. This creates the eyeholes, yet allows for the drama of the colored paper eye.

3. Glue on the nose and eyes, and continue the creation of the mask.

Staple yarn or ribbon to each side when the mask is finished. See BIRD MASKS, page 85, for more specific instructions. Inexpensive mask elastics may also be used.

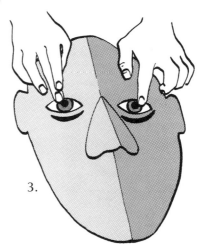

3.

Hand-Held Masks: Animal Faces

MATERIALS

For one mask . . .

    Construction paper
- At least one sheet, 12" x 18"
- Two or three sheets of 9" x 12" paper for some of the masks
- Several sheets of 6" x 9" paper in a variety of colors for features

Elmer's Glue-All

Pencil

Scissors

Hand-Held Stapler

A White Paper Plate, 9" in diameter

A Cardboard Rod from a Clothes Hanger

Masking Tape

Optional:
   X-acto Knife

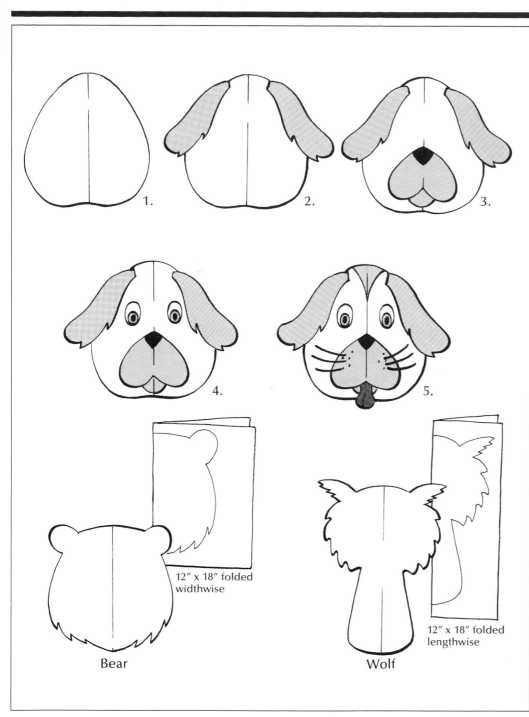

1.

2.

3.

4.

5.

12" x 18" folded widthwise

Bear

12" x 18" folded lengthwise

Wolf

Making an animal face is similar, in many ways, to making a human face. If, by chance, you've skipped to this section without glancing through PAPER WORKING TECHNIQUES and HUMAN FACES, take a moment to look through those sections before continuing.

An animal face can be divided into five major parts: 1. Basic Head Shape; 2. Ears; 3. Nose, Muzzle and Mouth; 4. Eyes; 5. Details.

BASIC HEAD SHAPE

Think of an animal. What is its head shape? Is it long, short, fat or wide?

To make a simple head shape, fold a piece of construction paper in half, widthwise or lengthwise, depending on the shape of the animal's head. Draw "half a head" from the folded side including the ear shapes if possible. Cut along the line and open. (Some mask designs, such as the monkey or elephant, need two pieces glued together to form the head shape. Try these after you've tried a basic one-piece head.)

Staple the sides of the mask to a 9" paper plate before adding any features. (See page 30.) If you plan to wear your mask, see page 43 for one method of cutting eyeholes.

Remember to save scraps. You'll be able to use them for other parts of the mask.

EARS

Think of the animal's ears. Are they long, skinny, pointed, rounded or floppy?

If the ears are too big to include in the basic head shape, cut two from a folded sheet of construction paper. Attach them with glue or staples to the head shape. As an added touch, cut the inner ear shapes from another color. Try scoring, folding or curling the ear shapes.

NOSE, MUZZLE AND MOUTH

Think of the animal's nose or muzzle. Is it pointed or flat? Is it wide or narrow?

To make a simple muzzle, fold a piece of paper and draw half the muzzle from the folded side. Cut out the muzzle and glue it to the face shape. Glue nose and mouth lines on the muzzle as shown in the illustration of the bear.

Another method is to cut a muzzle, lower lip and nose from separate pieces of paper. Slightly raise the muzzle (like a mountain) before gluing. Place a dab of glue on the creased edge of the lower lip, and slide it under the muzzle. (The direction of the lower lip fold is opposite that of the muzzle and head to give more dimension to the mask. See the raccoon on page 50.) The nose also can be slightly raised before gluing.

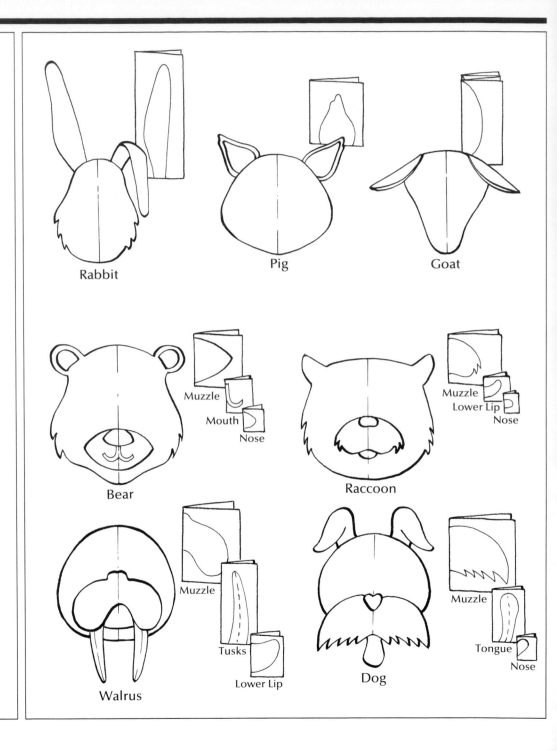

Rabbit

Pig

Goat

Bear

Muzzle

Mouth

Nose

Raccoon

Muzzle

Lower Lip

Nose

Walrus

Muzzle

Tusks

Lower Lip

Dog

Muzzle

Tongue

Nose

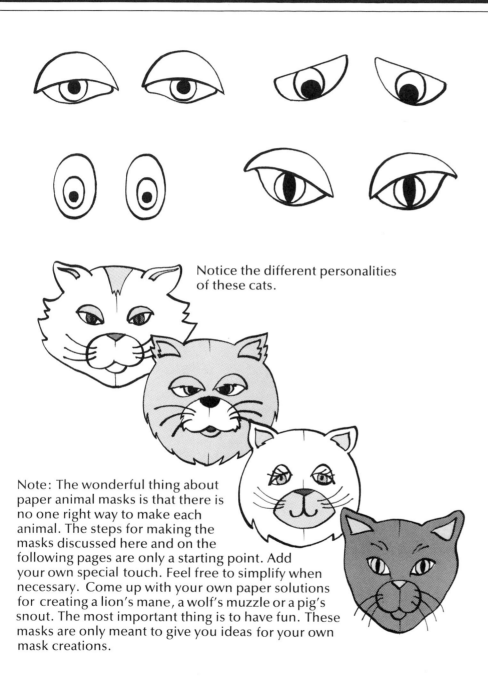

Notice the different personalities of these cats.

Note: The wonderful thing about paper animal masks is that there is no one right way to make each animal. The steps for making the masks discussed here and on the following pages are only a starting point. Add your own special touch. Feel free to simplify when necessary. Come up with your own paper solutions for creating a lion's mane, a wolf's muzzle or a pig's snout. The most important thing is to have fun. These masks are only meant to give you ideas for your own mask creations.

Some noses or muzzles require a few more steps, as with the pig, monkey and wolf. See the specific animal in the following section for more details.

EYES

Think of the animal's eyes. The size, shape and positioning of the eyes can tell a lot about the personality of the animal. First, think of the general shape of the eyes. Are they large, small, round, oval or almond-shaped? Cut an eyeball-iris-pupil combination. (See page 32 for details.)

Next, experiment with positioning. Eyes with the outer corners slanting down can give the animal a tired or sad expression. Eyes with the iris and pupil completely showing can make the animal appear surprised. Eyes with the outer corners slanting up can make the animal look more fierce.

You may want to add lids and eyelashes. (See pages 32 and 33 on human eyes for more details.)

Note: The pupil of a human eye is always round. The pupil of a cat eye can be round, or it can be a vertical almond shape.

DETAILS

Think of what makes your animal special (its distinguishing characteristics):
stripes; tusks; whiskers; spots; horns; manes.

Decorate as appropriate.

RACCOONS

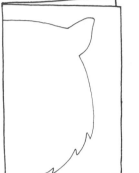

Cut the head shape from a 12" x 18" sheet of paper folded widthwise and attach to a paper plate. Cut the muzzle, lower lip and nose. Spot glue the muzzle in a raised position. Slide the lower lip into place. Glue the crease of the lower lip to the crease of the basic shape.

Basic Shape

Muzzle

Lower Lip

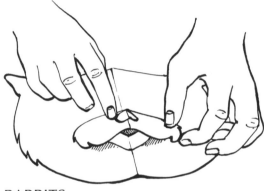

Add the large, black eye shapes and forehead markings which are the distinguishing characteristics of a raccoon.

RABBITS

Cut the head shape of the rabbit and staple to a paper plate. Cut and glue the muzzle, lower lip and nose in the same manner as the raccoon.

Cut the ears from a 12" x 18" sheet of paper folded lengthwise. Glue or staple to the head shape. Try scoring the ears. Try folding or curling for a flop-eared effect. An inner ear color can be added.

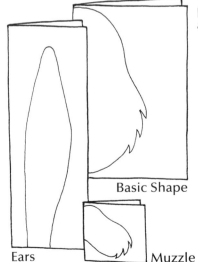

Basic Shape

Ears

Muzzle

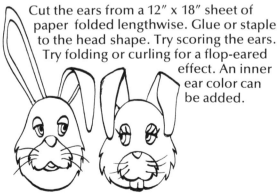

Don't forget the whiskers.

BEARS

There's no one right way to make an animal mask. For instance, here are two ways to make a bear.

As shown on the bear at the top, the nose and mouth lines are glued to the muzzle.

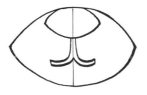

Nose   Mouth Lines

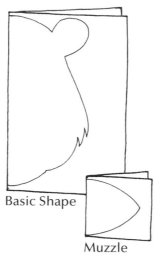

Basic Shape

Muzzle

The second bear has a muzzle, lower lip and nose similar to the raccoon or rabbit.

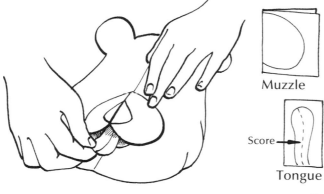

Muzzle

Score →

Tongue

The scored tongue is glued between the muzzle and the lower lip.

Lower Lip

DOGS

Each dog on this page begins with a circle or oval shape that is attached to a paper plate. To create the muzzle of the dog at the top, cut the muzzle shape, run a bead of glue along the edges as shown, and glue in a raised position on the face. Add a curled or scored tongue under the muzzle. A lower lip is optional.

Basic Shape

Glue

Muzzle

Ears

Muzzle

Ears

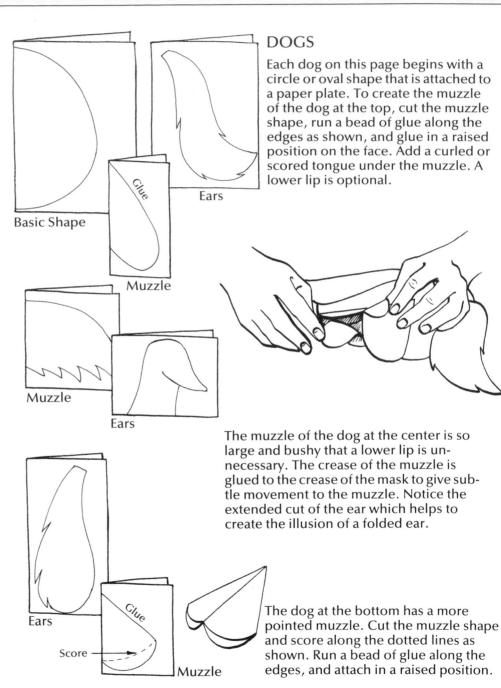

The muzzle of the dog at the center is so large and bushy that a lower lip is unnecessary. The crease of the muzzle is glued to the crease of the mask to give subtle movement to the muzzle. Notice the extended cut of the ear which helps to create the illusion of a folded ear.

Ears

Score

Glue

Muzzle

The dog at the bottom has a more pointed muzzle. Cut the muzzle shape and score along the dotted lines as shown. Run a bead of glue along the edges, and attach in a raised position.

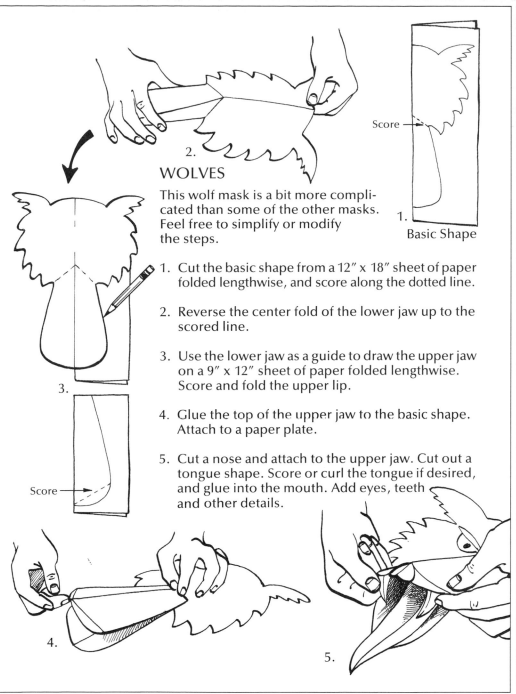

WOLVES

This wolf mask is a bit more complicated than some of the other masks. Feel free to simplify or modify the steps.

1. Cut the basic shape from a 12" x 18" sheet of paper folded lengthwise, and score along the dotted line.

2. Reverse the center fold of the lower jaw up to the scored line.

3. Use the lower jaw as a guide to draw the upper jaw on a 9" x 12" sheet of paper folded lengthwise. Score and fold the upper lip.

4. Glue the top of the upper jaw to the basic shape. Attach to a paper plate.

5. Cut a nose and attach to the upper jaw. Cut out a tongue shape. Score or curl the tongue if desired, and glue into the mouth. Add eyes, teeth and other details.

Basic Shape

Score

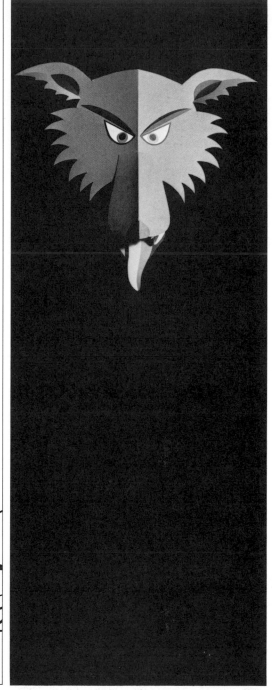

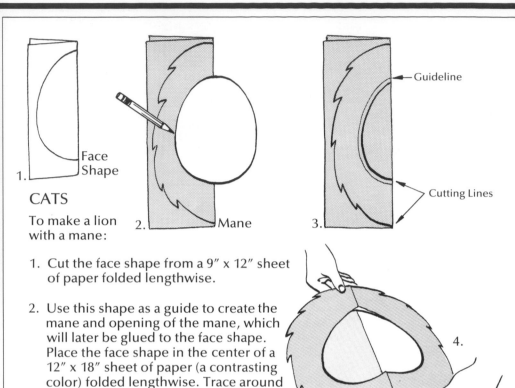

1. Face Shape

2. Mane

3. Guideline — Cutting Lines

CATS

To make a lion with a mane:

1. Cut the face shape from a 9" x 12" sheet of paper folded lengthwise.

2. Use this shape as a guide to create the mane and opening of the mane, which will later be glued to the face shape. Place the face shape in the center of a 12" x 18" sheet of paper (a contrasting color) folded lengthwise. Trace around the face shape. Draw the shape of the mane, and cut it out.

3. Cut the opening in the mane ½" beyond the guideline as shown. Staple the face shape to a paper plate.

4.

4. Glue the mane to the face shape.

Score — Extended Cut — Score — Wedge Shape

Nose

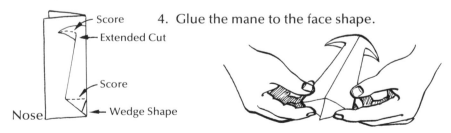

5. For the lion's nose, draw this shape on a 6" x 9" sheet of paper folded lengthwise. Cut out the wedge shape and score along the dotted lines.

6. Fold on the scored lines. Overlap the front nose tabs and glue.

7. Trace around the end of the nose on a dark color. Cut out the triangular shape.

8. Glue the triangular shape onto the tip of the nose.

Don't let all these directions intimidate you. A simple triangle can make an effective cat nose, too.

9. Cut out the lower lip and muzzle. Glue the nose, lower lip and muzzle as shown. (Remember not to glue the pieces down flat.) Finish by adding the eyes and ears.

Change your animal's personality by varying the size, shape and position of the individual features.

The lioness and tiger are similar to the lion. Simply add ears to the basic lion shape and skip the directions for the mane. Add stripes to distinguish a tiger from a lioness.

For the cat mask, use a muzzle similar to the raccoon or rabbit. Notice the jagged edges added to the cat at the lower right to create the illusion of fur. A tongue can be added between the lower lip and muzzle.

All cats have whiskers!

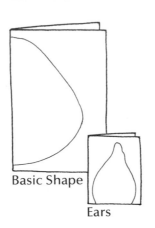

Basic Shape

Ears

PIGS

Pigs need to have a full, round, "porky" look. To achieve this, start with a fat oval, fuller on one end. Cut this from a 12" x 18" sheet of paper folded widthwise and staple it to a paper plate.

Add the wide ears, perhaps accenting them with an inner ear color. Cut circles for fat cheeks. (See page 36 for details.) Glue on the snout and eyes.

For a simple snout, glue a circular shape to the center of the face and add nostrils.

Directions for a more complicated snout follow.

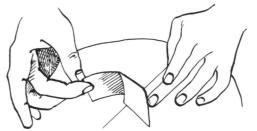

1. Cut the upper snout piece.

2. Curl slightly. Glue the longer side to the face shape.

3. Cut the lower snout piece.

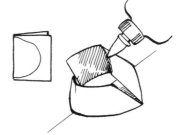

4. Curl slightly. Glue beneath the upper snout.

5. Cut out the tip of the nose. Run a bead of glue on the top edge of the upper snout.

6. Attach the tip of the nose. Add the nostril shapes.

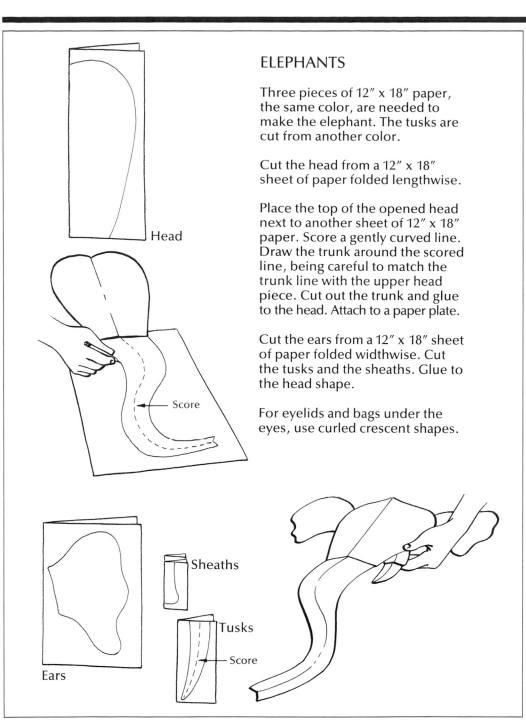

ELEPHANTS

Three pieces of 12″ x 18″ paper, the same color, are needed to make the elephant. The tusks are cut from another color.

Cut the head from a 12″ x 18″ sheet of paper folded lengthwise.

Place the top of the opened head next to another sheet of 12″ x 18″ paper. Score a gently curved line. Draw the trunk around the scored line, being careful to match the trunk line with the upper head piece. Cut out the trunk and glue to the head. Attach to a paper plate.

Cut the ears from a 12″ x 18″ sheet of paper folded widthwise. Cut the tusks and the sheaths. Glue to the head shape.

For eyelids and bags under the eyes, use curled crescent shapes.

Head

Score

Sheaths

Tusks

Score

Ears

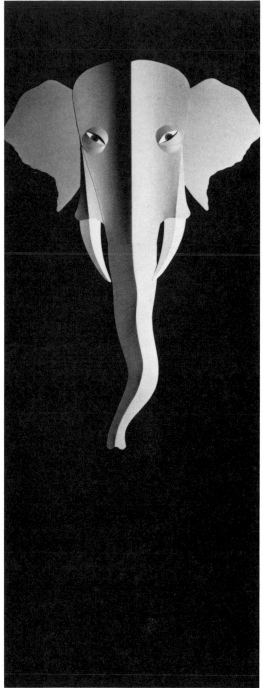

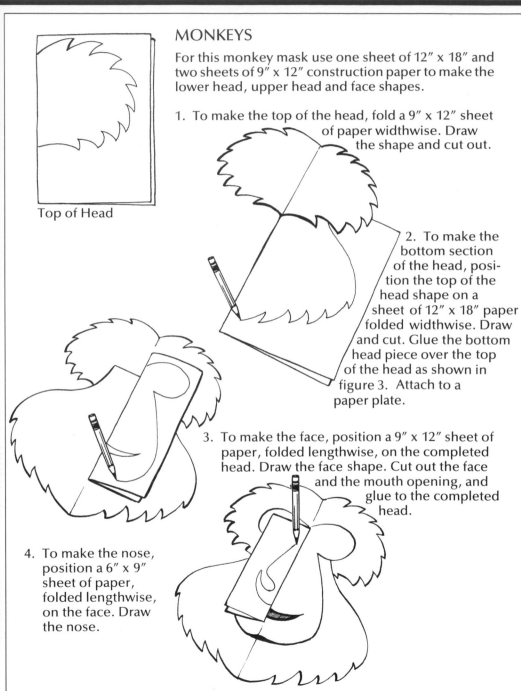

Top of Head

MONKEYS

For this monkey mask use one sheet of 12″ x 18″ and two sheets of 9″ x 12″ construction paper to make the lower head, upper head and face shapes.

1. To make the top of the head, fold a 9″ x 12″ sheet of paper widthwise. Draw the shape and cut out.

2. To make the bottom section of the head, position the top of the head shape on a sheet of 12″ x 18″ paper folded widthwise. Draw and cut. Glue the bottom head piece over the top of the head as shown in figure 3. Attach to a paper plate.

3. To make the face, position a 9″ x 12″ sheet of paper, folded lengthwise, on the completed head. Draw the face shape. Cut out the face and the mouth opening, and glue to the completed head.

4. To make the nose, position a 6″ x 9″ sheet of paper, folded lengthwise, on the face. Draw the nose.

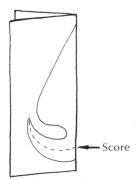

5. Cut out the nose, and score as shown.

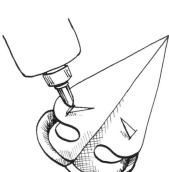

6. Bend on the scored lines and bring the tips up to the side of the nose. Use an X-acto knife to cut slits as shown. (The slit position will vary according to the size and shape of the nostrils.)

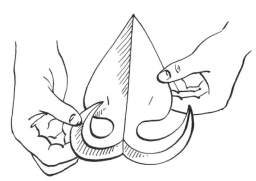

7. Insert the points and spot glue on the reverse side of the nose. Trim the tips.

8. Run a bead of glue along the edges of the nose that will make contact with the mask. Place the nose in position on the face. Add eyes and eyelids.

This is probably the most complicated construction in the book. A very simple monkey can be made from two circles and a button nose.

The bison, horse, goat and cow have several features in common. Compare the nose shapes of the bison, horse and goat with the monkey nose from the previous page. Notice the similarities of the horns of the bison, goat and cow. In addition, all four animals have ears and forelocks which can be made in a variety of ways.

BISON

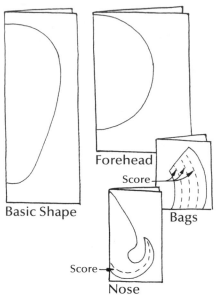

Basic Shape

Forehead

Score

Bags

Score

Nose

For the bison, begin with the basic head cut from a 12" x 18" sheet of paper folded lengthwise. Cut the forehead from a 12" x 18" sheet folded widthwise. Glue this to the head shape. Attach to a paper plate. Add the nose, eyes, ears and horns. Bags under the eyes may be scored as indicated and glued in place.

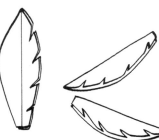

Ears

One way to create ears is to cut two from a folded sheet of paper. Score and notch as desired. Another way is to cut a pair of ears from *two* folded sheets *at the same time.* Open the ears and place them on top of each other. Notch one side. (Reverse the fold of one ear before attaching to the head.)

HORSES

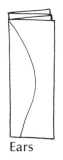

Score

Basic Shape

The basic head shape of the horse includes the nostrils. Fold a piece of 12" x 18" paper lengthwise. Cut out this shape. Score and complete nostrils (see monkey nose for details). Attach to a paper plate. Add the ears, eyes and finishing details.

GOATS

Cut the basic head shape of the goat from a 12" x 18" sheet of paper folded lengthwise. Attach to a paper plate.

Add the nose, eyes, ears, horns, beard and other details.

The goat nose is the same as the bison or monkey nose.

Cut the chin shape and glue it under the lower edge of the face shape. Cut several layers of long, fringed pieces, and glue them under the chin to form a beard. The strands may be scored and curled for added dimension.

Ears for both the cow and the goat are cut in the manner described on the preceding page. The scored horns are glued to the front of the basic shape. Several scored crescent shapes are glued together to form forelocks.

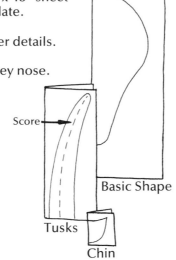

Score

Basic Shape

Tusks

Chin

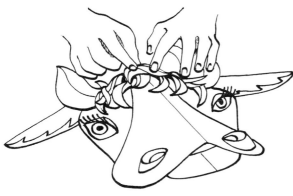

COWS

Cut the basic head shape of the cow and attach it to a paper plate. Cut and glue the nose (minus the nostrils) onto the basic head shape. A lower lip is optional.

The nostrils are scored crescents which are glued at the tips before they are attached to the nose. (Directions for this crescent shape can be found on page 63.)

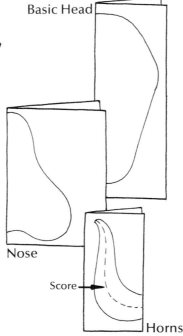

Basic Head

Nose

Score

Horns

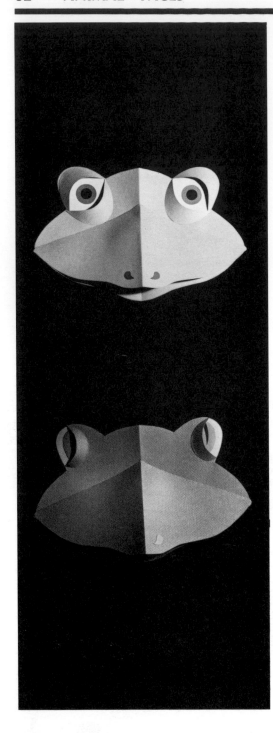

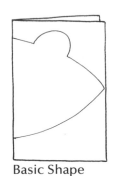

Upper Jaw

Lower Jaw

Basic Shape

FROGS

Two pieces of 9" x 12" paper folded width-wise are needed to make this frog.

1. Draw and cut the basic shape from the first folded sheet. Draw the upper and lower jaw shapes from the second sheet. Notice that the basic shape and the upper jaw are the same width. The lower jaw shape is slightly smaller.

2. Glue the top of the upper jaw to the basic head shape.

3. Slip in the lower jaw and glue at the corners only to form a mouth. Attach to a paper plate.

Add the eyes and other finishing details. Curled crescents may be used for eyelids.

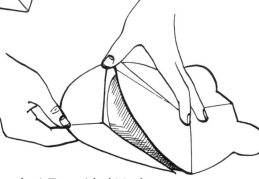

Optional: A Two-sided Mask

To create a two-sided frog mask, make two paper masks the same size, but do not attach to paper plates. Tape a rod to the back of one mask. Glue the two faces together back-to-back.

Remember: Two-sided masks aren't limited to frogs.

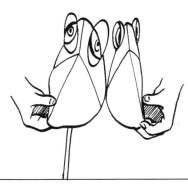

WALRUSES

Cut the basic head shape of the walrus from a 12" x 18" sheet of paper folded widthwise and attach to a paper plate.

The muzzle of the walrus is similar to a dog, bear, rabbit or raccoon.

The tusks can be scored and added between the muzzle and the lower lip.

An interesting eye shape can be created from scored crescents which are joined at the tips, then glued over the eyes.

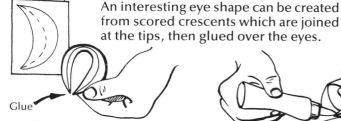

Glue

Basic Shape

Muzzle

Lower Lip

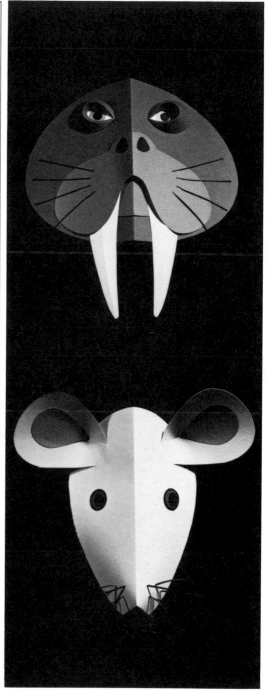

MICE

Draw and cut the basic head shape from a 12" x 18" sheet of paper folded widthwise. Cut out the wedge at the bottom of the basic shape. Score along the lines indicated. Overlap and glue the tabs to make a triangle shape for the nose. Add a small triangle of another color for the tip of the nose. Attach the mask to a paper plate.

Ears can be glued to the front or back of the head. To make ears similar to the example shown, cut out two ear shapes. Cut a slit at the base of each ear as shown. Overlap the tabs and glue. This creates extra dimension. Cut slits in the basic head shape. Insert the ears from the front. Glue the inserted tabs to the back of the mask.

Add eyes and finishing details.

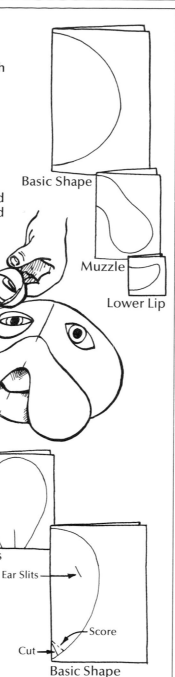

Ears

Ear Slits

Score

Cut

Basic Shape

Fish Marionettes

MATERIALS

For one fish marionette . . .

Construction paper
- Two sheets of the same color, 12" x 18"
- Several sheets in a variety of colors, 6" x 9" or scraps for features and decorations

Elmer's Glue-All

Pencil

Scissors

Hand-Held Stapler

A Cardboard Rod from a Clothes Hanger

Yarn or Carpet Thread with Needle

Facial Tissue

Optional: X-acto Knife

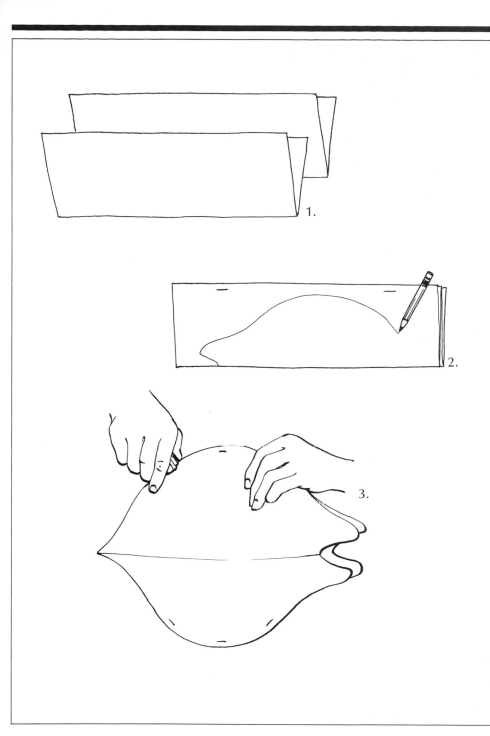

BASIC SHAPE

1. Fold the two pieces of 12" x 18" construction paper (same color) in half, lengthwise.

2. Match up the folded edges and put two staples on the outside edge to hold the paper in place when cutting.

   Draw one half of a fish body from the folded edge.

   Cut out the shape.

3. Open.

   Turn one of the sides over so that both mountain folds are on the outside.

   Match up the edges of the fish.

   Put three staples on the top and three staples on the bottom about ½" from the edge.

TAIL

Decide on the shape of the tail. Fold a 6" x 9" sheet of construction paper in half and cut out half of a tail from the fold. Decorate as desired.

Insert the tail into the back end of the fish and glue.

DORSAL FIN

Lay the fish marionette on a sheet of 6" x 9" construction paper with most of the paper showing. Draw a line on the paper around the back. This line will be the bottom of the dorsal fin, which will fit into the back of the fish body.

Draw the top part of the dorsal fin. Cut out, insert and spot glue between the sides of the fish's back.

You may want to cut a matching fin at the same time for the bottom of the fish.

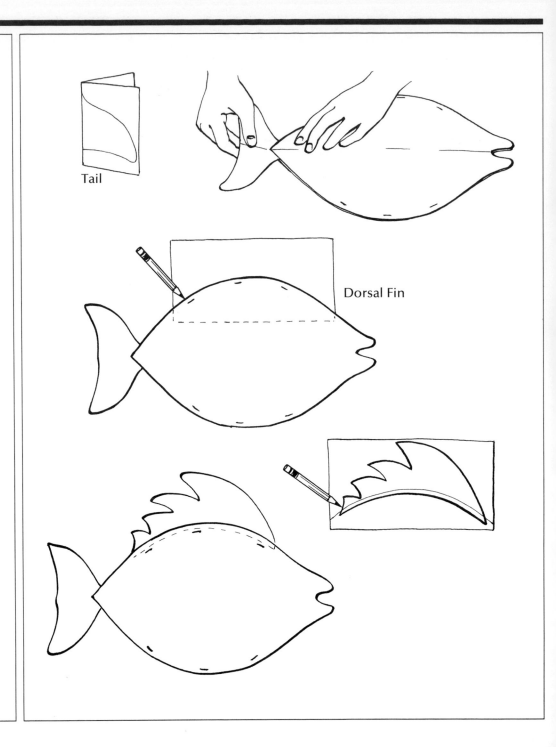

Tail

Dorsal Fin

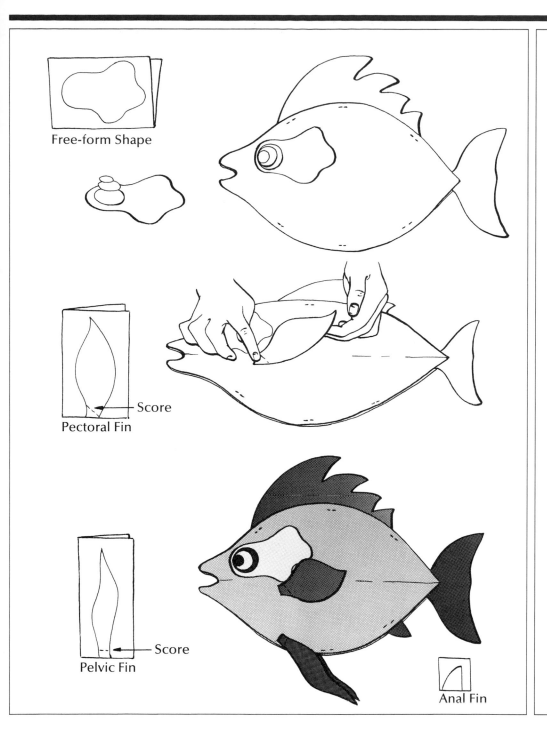

Free-form Shape

Score

Pectoral Fin

Score

Pelvic Fin

Anal Fin

EYES

Use three colors for the eyes (eye-ball, iris and pupil). For added design, cut two free-form shapes from a folded 6" x 9" sheet of construction paper.

Glue the eyeball-iris-pupil combination to each shape and then glue each shape to the fish's body. (Look down the snout of the fish for correct positioning of the eye shapes.)

ADDITIONAL FINS

Fish have two **pectoral fins**. They are like arms and are located toward the front of the fish. Cut the fins from a folded sheet of 6" x 9" paper. Score and fold a small connecting tab at the base of each fin. Put a dab of glue on the tab to attach a fin to each side of the fish.

The two **pelvic fins** are like legs and are located on the lower portion of the fish's body. Cut two fins, score and fold connecting tabs and glue a fin to each side of the body.

The **anal fin** is a single fin located at the bottom of the fish near the tail. Cut it from a single sheet of paper, insert and spot glue between the two sides of the fish.

GILLS

Cut two crescent shapes from a folded piece of paper to make gills.

Glue one to each side.

DETAILS

Decorate your fish marionette with interesting designs. Use stripes, dots, abstract shapes . . .

ATTACHING THE STRINGS

Use two pieces of yarn or carpet thread to attach the fish to the rod. One piece is stapled near the snout – one is stapled near the tail. (Bring the short end of the yarn back across the staple, and staple again, to lock the yarn in place.)

Older children can use carpet thread and a needle when stringing their marionettes. Again, thread is attached near the snout and near the tail. Attach string by tying instead of stapling. Care must be taken in tying the knot so as not to damage the construction paper. Add a drop of glue to the knot to secure it.

Tie the strings to a clothes hanger rod by looping through a notch at the end of the rod and winding the string around several times before tying the knot.

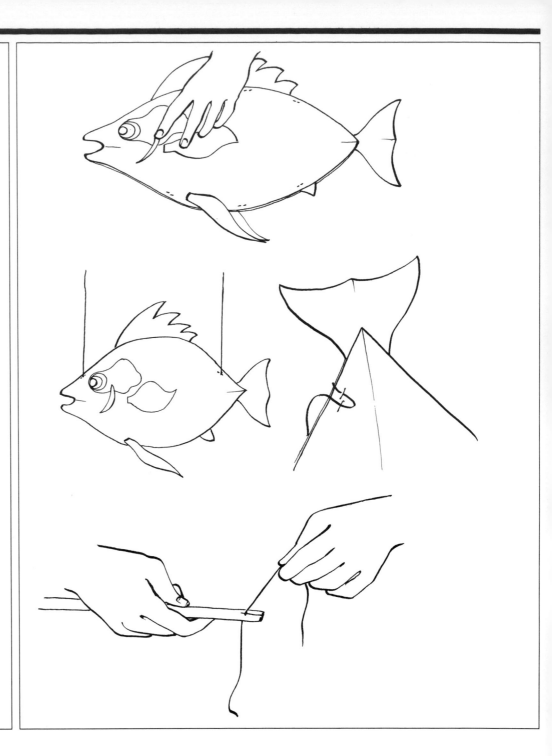

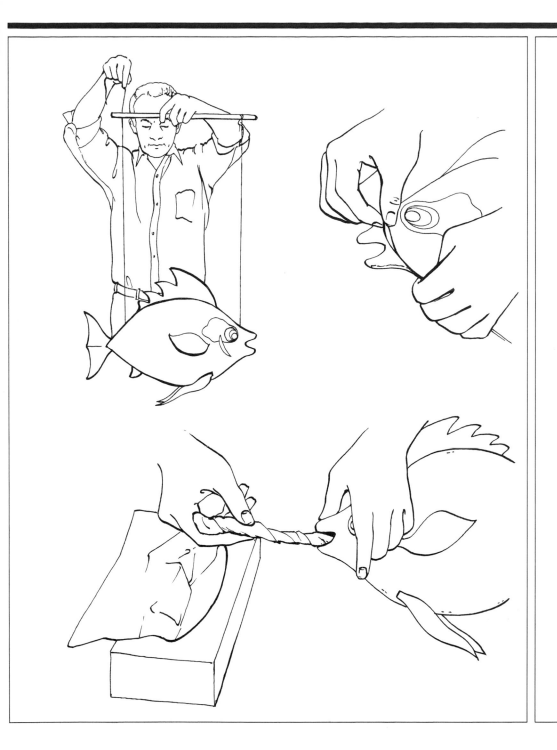

When tying the second string, make sure the fish is parallel to the rod.

To give the fish body more fullness, seal the top and bottom parts of the jaw with Elmer's Glue.

When the glue is dry, stuff the fish with facial tissue. Feed fish gently.

Mask Mobiles

MATERIALS

For one mask mobile . . .

Construction paper
- Two sheets, 12" x 18", contrasting colors
- Several sheets of 6" x 9" paper in a variety of colors for features

Elmer's Glue-All

Pencil

Scissors

Hand-Held Stapler

Thin Yarn or Carpet Thread with Needle

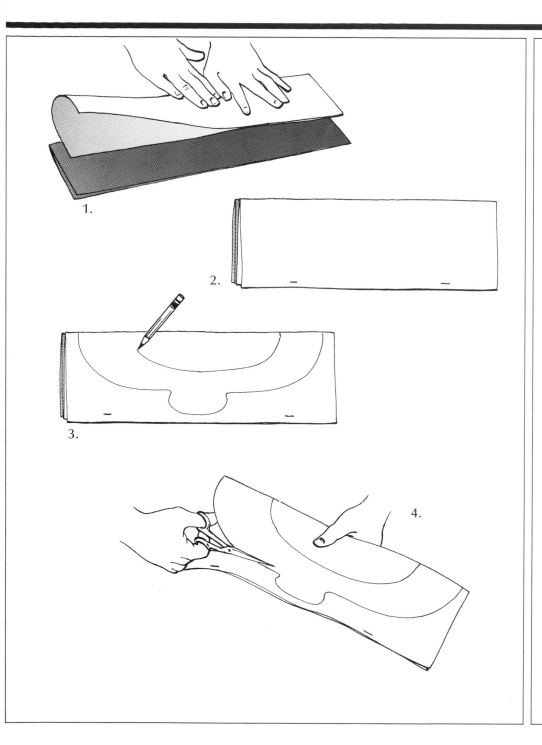

BASIC SHAPE

1. Fold two pieces of 12" x 18" construction paper (contrasting colors) in half, lengthwise or widthwise.

2. Match up the folded edges and put two staples on the outside edge.

3. Draw half a face and an oval shape on the folded edge.

4. Cut out the face and the oval shape.

5. Open. (There will be two exact
    shapes of different colors.)

    Glue back-to-back . . .

    or . . .

    cut one shape in half and glue
    a half on each side of the uncut
    shape to create an alternating
    dark-light effect. (Note: Be
    sure the second piece has the
    glue on the correct side. Test
    before applying glue.)

The following steps emphasize the
dark-light pattern. It is only one
of many design ideas for a mask
mobile. Experiment with some of
your own.

NOSE AND EYES

With the leftover ovals from the
center of the face, cut out a nose-
eye combination from the fold.
Again, cut one in half and glue to
each side of the uncut shape.

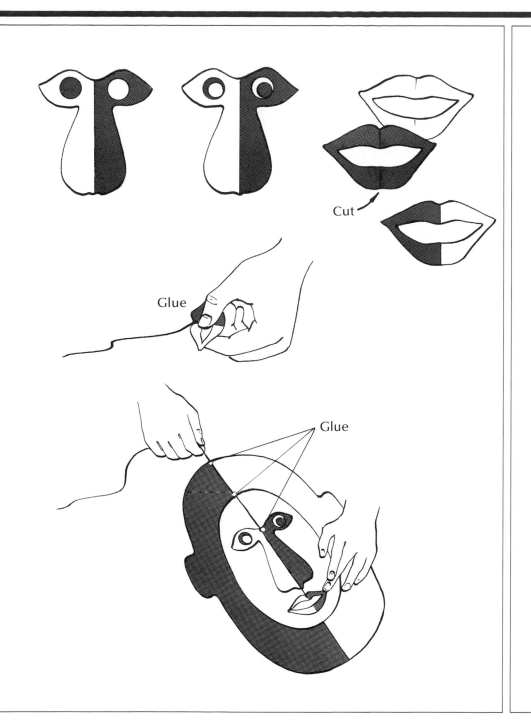

Cut

Glue

Glue

The eye area of this shape is the base for the iris and the pupil. Alternate as shown.

MOUTH

Cut two mouths from two pieces of folded scrap. Alternate as shown.

DETAILS

Some of the following details may be added to your mobile: hair, eyebrows, eyelids, mustaches, cheeks, hats and bows.

Continue to alternate colors on opposite sides of the mobile.

ATTACHING THE STRING

Use one continuous piece of thin yarn or carpet thread to string the mobile.

Attach yarn or carpet thread in the following places: top of lip, top of brow, forehead and top of head.

Use a small hand-held stapler and/or Elmer's Glue-All for attaching the yarn or carpet thread.

Bird Masks

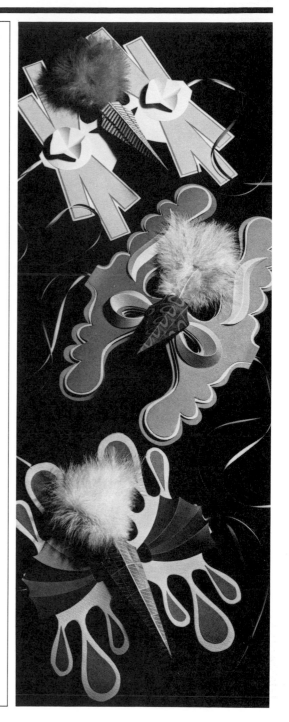

MATERIALS

For one bird mask . . .

Construction paper
- One sheet, 12″ x 18″
- Several sheets of 6″ x 9″ paper in a variety of colors for features

Elmer's Glue-All

Pencil

Scissors

Hand-Held Stapler

Yarn

Paper Towel Square

Crayons

Optional:
   X-acto Knife
   Feathers
   Cellophane
   Glitter
   Sequins
   Masking Tape

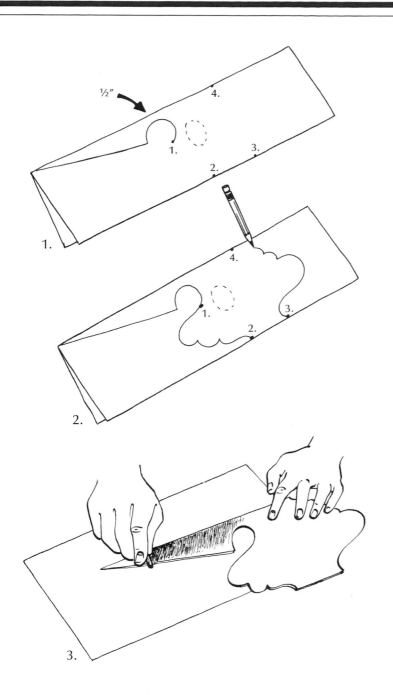

BASIC SHAPE

To make a bird mask, a piece of 12" x 18" construction paper is needed.

1. For younger children, an adult or older child can fold the paper and draw the beak and hook shape, as shown, ahead of time. Four guide marks should also be made at this time.

2. Have each child draw an interesting line from the end of the drawn hook #1 to point #2. Then connect points #3 and #4 with another interesting line. Children should be careful not to draw the line into the future eye area.

Older children can draw the beak, hook shape and interesting lines on their own.

Cut out the shape.

3. To give the beak a contrasting color, place the beak on a paper towel and, with the side of a crayon, gently color each side of the beak. Be sure to get color above the hook shape. Several colors may be used, one on top of the other, or patterns may be drawn.

Another way of adding a contrasting color to the beak is to fold a piece of construction paper in half and trace the beak of the mask on the fold. Cut out and glue to the beak of the mask.

4. Fold the beak across the mask. Reverse the fold of the mask. (Note: The back side of the mask now becomes the front side. This will hide any "goofs" made while drawing the interesting lines of step 2.)

5. Set the beak at the desired angle and crease well at the top to hold it in the desired position.

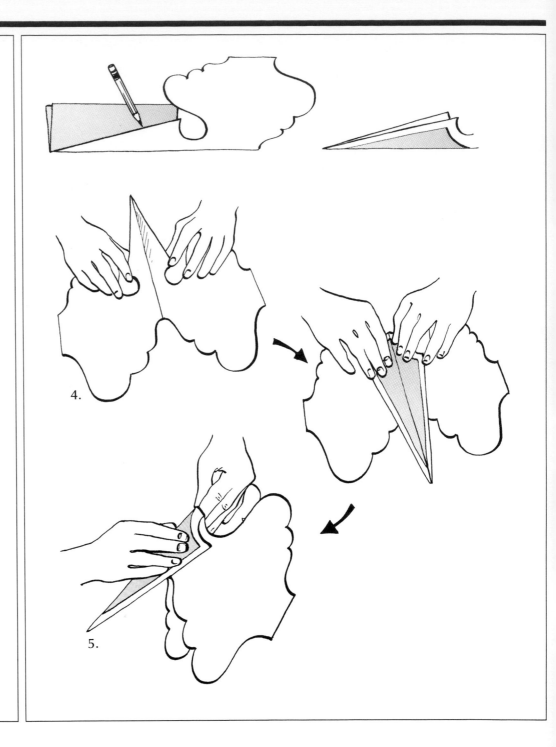

4.

5.

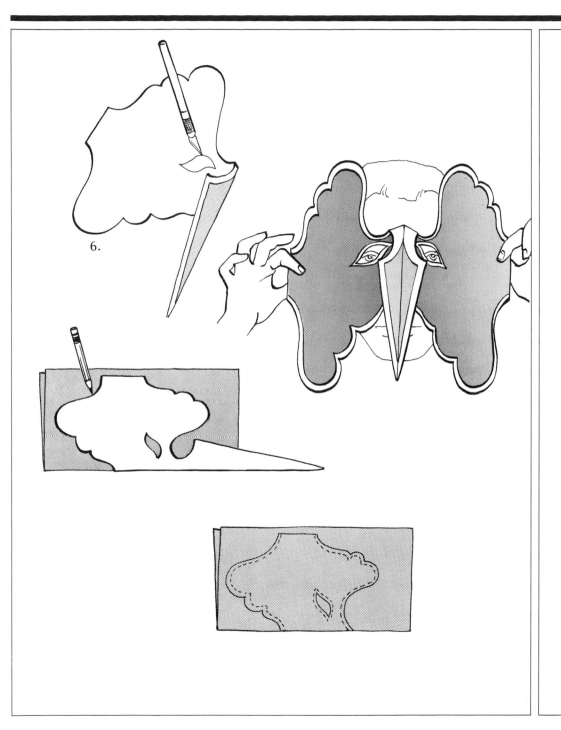

6.

6. Hold the mask to the face to determine the approximate location of the eye holes.

Fold the mask in half and cut out eyes with scissors, or use an X-acto knife and cutting board. (Note: Interesting shapes can be cut quickly with an X-acto knife, but be careful!)

DETAILS

Here are some ways of making your bird mask more fanciful.

Add a second color by tracing the basic mask shape on a folded 9" x 12" sheet of paper. Cut the second mask shape slightly smaller as shown by the dotted lines in the illustration. Glue this shape on the front of the mask.

To add an interesting topknot try the following:

Fringe and curl paper.

Add brightly colored feathers such as marabou fluffs for a dramatic effect. Secure the base of several feathers with masking tape. Glue the taped feathers to the back fold of the beak.

Add interesting patterns and designs by making simple flat shapes, scored shapes and curled shapes – all cut from paper. (Start with larger shapes first; add smaller details last.)

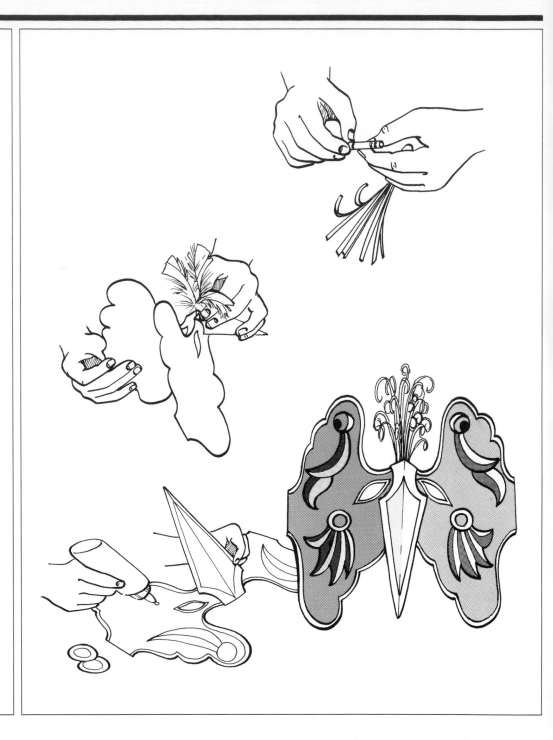

To create a colored world, place colored cellophane squares behind the eyeholes and attach them with masking tape around the edges. Be sure the tape secures **all** the edges.

Add glitter or sequins to make sparkling designs **only** if cellophane squares have been attached securely to make sure the eyes are protected. Keep the glitter contained in a box to avoid a "sparkling" mess.

ATTACHING THE STRINGS

Use two pieces of yarn, each about 6" in length.

Turn the mask over.

Staple one piece of yarn about an inch in from the outside edge.

Fold the short end over and staple again. (This locks the yarn in place.)

Staple the other piece of yarn to the other side in the same manner.

Elastic from a fabric store or mask elastics from a display and costume shop may be used in place of yarn.

Stories, Songs and Plays

MATERIALS

For group stories, radio plays and songs . . .

Chalkboard or Clipboard

Chalk or Pencil

Tape Recorder

Blank Tape for Recording

Optional:
    Musical Instruments
    Rhythm Instruments
    Sound Effects

For plays . . .

Masks or Puppets

Optional:
    Musical Instruments
    Sound Effects
    Props
    Costumes

GROUP STORIES

Ideas for writing stories flow more easily when children have a strong interest in the characters. Making masks, marionettes or mobiles is a good way to motivate that interest. Once children have made the characters, the leader can use the following suggestions to create a group story.

1. Discuss the elements of a good story: characters, setting and plot.

2. Select the characters.
   - ☐ The masks or puppets that have just been completed will become the main characters in the story.
   - ☐ Discuss the characters to develop their personalities.

3. Decide on a setting for the story.
   - ☐ Mask or puppet characters will often determine the setting.
   - ☐ Allow enough time to paint a detailed "word picture" of the setting.
   - ☐ Possible questions:
     "What does it look like?"
     "What are the characters doing?"
     "What sounds do you hear?"

4. Begin the story.
   - ☐ Using ideas from the discussion of the setting, start the story.
   - ☐ Possible beginnings:
     "It was a stormy night on the mountain where the trolls lived."
     "All of the fish were swimming happily around the bright coral when . . ."
     "Bimbo, the clown, was setting up his circus tent."

5. Develop the plot.
   - ☐ Let the events of the story unfold. This is where the action takes place or where problems are introduced.
   - ☐ Get ideas from as many people in the group as possible.
   - ☐ Listen, ask open-ended questions, encourage and give support.

6. Jot the story line on a chalkboard or a clipboard as it develops.

7. Keep in mind that every story should have a satisfying conclusion.

Here is an example of a story written by Mrs. Rush's third grade class in Zillah, Washington, after the children had finished making masks of all kinds of people.

MATT AND HIS MASK MAKERS

Once upon a time, there was a mask maker named Matt. He wasn't very rich. He wore raggedy clothes and a floppy painter's hat. He carried an old suitcase covered with patches. Inside the suitcase were all his materials – paper, scissors, glue, paints and paint brushes.

One day Matt was riding his horse toward the castle because the king wanted him to come make some masks. When he got to the castle, the drawbridge came down, and Matt rode his horse right onto the castle grounds.

When the king saw the mask maker, he came out and said, "Do you have all your things?"

Matt said, "Yes, your Majesty. What kind of masks do you want?"

The king said, "I want paper masks . . . some animals, some like a princess, some like a prince, some that look very funny and one dragon mask 16 feet long with paper fire."

Now, the king wanted all these masks because there was going to be a grand celebration. The prince had recently married and he was now going to be crowned the new king.

When Matt heard of all the masks that the king wanted, he said, "Your Majesty, how much time do I have?"

The king said, "You have three days."

Matt said, "Oh, no! May I get some help?"

The king answered, "Yes, of course."

So Matt went into the village and asked some people to help him. He found an old carpenter, a young girl, a shoemaker, a teacher, a weaver, a tailor and a very old man. He asked them if they would like to help him make some masks, and they all said, "Yes."

Matt got everyone together and taught them how to make masks. They worked for three days and got them ready just in time for the celebration.

When the king saw the masks, he said, "These masks are fit for a king, and I want all you mask makers to wear them in the parade."

Everyone cheered!

The king gave the mask maker some money, new clothes, a new suitcase, and, of course, more materials for making masks. He said to Matt, "You may come back to **this** castle **any time!**"

RADIO PLAYS

After a group story has been written, it is an excellent time to turn the story into a "radio play" – a tape-recorded version of the story.

1. Sequence the events of the story.

2. Discuss where sound effects can be added to the story:
   - ☐ creaking door
   - ☐ telephone ringing
   - ☐ rainstorm
   - ☐ crackling fire
   - ☐ birds singing

3. Assign character parts.

4. Choose a narrator for the story.

5. Add background music:
   - ☐ piano, autoharp, guitar, recorder . . .
   - ☐ recordings that suit the mood of the story

6. Rehearse.

7. Tape record.

8. Listen and enjoy!

This is how MATT AND HIS MASK MAKERS was turned into a radio play. Imagine the fun everyone had listening to the finished product. (This script was also used, later, when the play was being rehearsed on stage.)

NARRATOR: Once upon a time, there was a mask maker named Matt. He wasn't very rich. He wore raggedy clothes and a floppy painter's hat. He carried an old suitcase covered with patches. Inside the suitcase were all his materials – paper, scissors, glue, paints and paint brushes.

One day Matt was riding his horse toward the castle because the king wanted him to come make some masks. *(Hoof beats fading out in background.)* When he got to the castle, the drawbridge came down, and Matt rode his horse right onto the castle grounds. *(Sound of drawbridge coming down . . . hoof beats.)*

When the king saw the mask maker, he came out and said,

KING: Do you have all your things?

MATT: Yes, your Majesty. What kind of masks do you want?

KING: I want paper masks . . . some animals, some like a princess, some like a prince, some that look very funny and one dragon mask 16 feet long with paper fire.

NARRATOR: Now, the king wanted all these masks because there was going to be a grand celebration. The prince had recently married and he was now going to be crowned the new king.

When Matt heard of all the masks that the king wanted, he said,

MATT: Your Majesty, how much time do I have?

KING: You have three days.

MATT: Oh, no! May I get some help?

KING: Yes, of course.

NARRATOR: So Matt went into the village and asked some people to help him. He found an old carpenter.

MATT: Will you help me make some masks?

CARPENTER: Yes, I will.

NARRATOR: He found a young girl and asked,

MATT: Will you help me make some masks?

YOUNG GIRL: Yes.

NARRATOR: He met a shoemaker and said,

MATT: Will you help me make some masks?

SHOEMAKER: Of course.

NARRATOR: Then he met a teacher . . .

MATT: Will you help me make some masks?

TEACHER: Yes, I will.

NARRATOR: Next, he found a weaver . . .

MATT: Will you help me make some masks?

WEAVER: Of course, I will.

NARRATOR: Then Matt came to a tailor . . .

MATT: Will you help me make some masks?

TAILOR: I'd be happy to help.

NARRATOR: And finally Matt met a very old man and said,

MATT: Will you help me make some masks?

OLD MAN: Yes, I will.

NARRATOR: Matt got everyone together and taught them how to make masks. They worked for three days and got them ready just in time for the celebration. *(Sound of people working, making masks.)* When the king saw the masks, he said,

KING: These masks are fit for a king, and I want all you mask makers to wear them in the parade. *(Everyone cheers.)*

NARRATOR: The king gave the mask maker some money, new clothes, a new suitcase, and, of course, more materials for making masks. He said to Matt:

KING: You may come to **this** castle **any time!**

SONGS

Writing songs can be fun when you have a group of people contributing ideas. Here are some suggestions to help take the mystery out of song writing. If you are trying this for the first time, you might want to have a musical friend help you.

1. Discuss the two main parts of a song:
    ☐ Lyrics – the words
    ☐ Melody – the tune

2. Make a "word bank" – a list of descriptive words about the topic on which you are writing.

3. Think of an opening line for the song.

4. Add more ideas to the opening line until you have the first verse.

5. If a rhyming pattern is desired:
    ☐ Talk about rhyming words.
    ☐ Find a way to make a rhyming pattern if one hasn't occurred naturally in the writing.

6. After the first verse has been written, read the lyrics together several times to find the rhythm.

7. Create a melody, line by line. Sing each line several times before adding a melody to the next line.
    (This repetition sets the melody and rhyming pattern.)

8. Write additional verses.
    ☐ Try to use ideas from all members of the group.
    ☐ Don't forget to look at the "word bank" for ideas.

9. Each time a new verse is written, sing the entire song again.
    (By the time the lyrics have been completed, everyone will know the song well enough to record.)

10. Tape record.

11. Listen and enjoy.

Here is an example of a song written by Mr. Maxfield's fourth grade class in Zillah, Washington, after they had made masks of fanciful zoo animals. Later they turned their song into an illustrated book.

THE MAGICAL DREAM

On a cloud there is a zoo. A zany, zany zoo.

All the animals dance & play, & blow star kisses to you ... And

blow star kisses to you.

1. On a cloud there is a zoo,
   A zany, zany zoo.
   All the animals dance and play,
   And blow star kisses to you . . .
   And blow star kisses to you.

2. All the golden cages glow,
   When there's a rainbow near.
   All the animals laugh and play,
   And that's what brought me
     here . . .
   And that's what brought me
     here.

3. All the dedfords jump and sing,
   And eat the chocolate grass.
   The kingles like to play
     hopscotch.
   Do you have a calico pass . . .
   Do you have a calico pass?

4. Yes, I have a calico pass.
   I got it from my dreams.
   I stepped through a magic door,
   And had some golden ice
     cream . . .
   And had some golden ice
     cream.

5. The animals were having a
     party, then,
   And they invited me.
   They were eating zany cake,
   And drinking magic tea . . .
   And drinking magic tea.

6. When I took a sip of tea,
   I woke up in my bed.
   This had been a magic dream
   That lived inside my head . . .
   That lived inside my head.

On a cloud there is a zoo

A zany, zany zoo.

The following step-by-step process was used to guide the children as they wrote THE MAGICAL DREAM. The same basic process can be used for writing other songs.

(The leader's comments are designated by **bold type**, the children's responses by *italicized type*.)

The basic elements of a song were discussed with the children.

Every song has lyrics and a melody, and the easiest way to write a song is to start with the lyrics.

Before writing the lyrics, the children came up with a list of descriptive words about their animals that were put into a "word bank."

beautiful	fly	clouds	striped
hop	chocolate	rainbow colors	kiss
magic	golden	dream	dedfords
dance	kingles	prance	play

The children were asked for an opening line for their song:

On a cloud there is a zoo.

Tell me more about the zoo.
A zany, zany zoo.

Tell me more about the animals.
All the animals dance and play.

In most songs, you find rhyming words. Can anyone find a way to make a rhyming pattern in this first verse?
And blow star kisses to you.

You could repeat the last line.
O.K. Great!

And blow star kisses to you.

After this first verse was written, the class read the lyrics together several times to find the rhythm.

Ón ă clóud thĕre ís ă zóo.
Ă zánў, zánў zóo.
Áll thĕ ánĭmăls dánce ănd pláy,
Ănd blów stăr kíssĕs tŏ yóu . . .
Ănd blów stăr kíssĕs tŏ yóu.

Before writing additional verses, a melody was written, line by line.

Does anyone have a melody he can hum that we could put with the first line of our poem? Anything you hum will work.
Hummed:

That's great! Let's put that melody with the words in the first line.

The first line was sung several times.

Who has another melody we could use in the second line?
Hummed:

Let's sing the second line.

The second line was sung several times.

Now, let's sing both the lines together.

The rest of the melody was written in the same manner.

When this was completed, the melody and the rhyming pattern were well-established.

It is important to mention that the children received lots of positive reinforcement while they were writing their song. By the time the first verse was written, everyone was enthusiastic about their new creation.

Additional verses were written, line by line, using ideas both from the word bank and from members of the group.

After each verse was written, it was sung.

Each time a new verse was written, the entire song was sung again.

By the time the lyrics were completed, everyone knew the song well enough to record.

All the animals dance and play

And blow star kisses to you.

PLAYS: STORIES IN PERFORMANCE

After children have made masks or puppets and have written a story, they are ready to create a play. Here are a few things to consider when turning a group story into a dramatic presentation.

1. Establish the space.

   ☐ In order to put on a play, you need space, but plays need not be confined to conventional spaces such as auditoriums and multipurpose rooms. Some rooms can easily be turned into a playing area by simply rearranging furniture. Some of the furniture can even be used in the set.

   ☐ If you have a large, empty space, use it.

2. Create the set.

   ☐ In the playing area, or set, firmly establish the various locations of the story.

   ☐ The set pieces like mountains or ponds can be imaginary, or they can be created from furniture in the room, large pieces of fabric or paper.

   ☐ Children can become important parts of the set by forming arches, rocks, trees or other necessary parts of the set.

3. Block out the play.

   ☐ Blocking is the arrangement of the characters in the set – how they move and where they move – their entrances and exits.

   ☐ It is essential that the group discuss the blocking before they begin rehearsing the play. They must know where they are going and why.

   ☐ Blocking also includes the handling of props, which, sometimes, takes practice.

4. Determine the method of presentation.

   ☐ Someone acts as a narrator and reads or tells the story as the group acts it out.

   ☐ One of the characters can tell the story in the first person while the other characters act it out.

   ☐ The story can be done as a puppet play using marionettes or hand-held masks as puppets.

   ☐ The story can be done in mime.

   ☐ It can even be presented as a musical.

5. Rehearse the play.

- ☐ Assign the roles:
  - ☐ leading characters
  - ☐ incidental characters
  - ☐ special effect technicians (music, sound effects, lighting . . .)
  - ☐ children as parts of a set
- ☐ Walk the group through the story so all the players are familiar with the blocking.
- ☐ Improvise the dialogue when it occurs spontaneously. It will add interest to the scene, and the actors will appear more relaxed and natural.
- ☐ Remind the children to use good diction and to project their voices so the audience can hear them.
- ☐ Decide where to use sound effects and music, either recorded or provided by individuals.
- ☐ Rehearse often. The more times the play is rehearsed, the better it will become.
- ☐ Provide encouragement for those children who will strive for a more polished theater production with elaborate props, sets and costumes. They can do this with your support.

6. Find an audience.

- ☐ If half the group is performing, the other half can be the audience. (If you have a large group, several smaller groups can perform the play for each other. It will be interesting to see the different versions of the same story.)
- ☐ In a school, other classes will make a good audience.
- ☐ Invite parents, grandparents, friends and neighbors.
- ☐ Take your show "on the road" to visit such places as neighboring schools, retirement centers, hospitals or shopping malls.

7. Make a video tape to become a permanent record of your performance.

8. Expand children's talents in producing an original play by:

- ☐ Designing a program
- ☐ Advertising
- ☐ Taking photographs
- ☐ Choreographing a dance
- ☐ Painting backdrops
- ☐ Creating a song
- ☐ Building props

SOME SPECIAL THOUGHTS ON USING MASKS:

☐ Children should keep their bodies positioned so that their masks are pointed in the general direction of the audience.

☐ In scenes where there are groups of characters around a table or a campfire, keep the front area open so the audience is not looking at the backs of the players.

☐ Each child should decide how he wants his character to move. Oftentimes, this happens spontaneously, but some children may be helped with guiding questions or statements such as:

"Show us some different ways your character can walk."

"Can your character do any tricks? Show us."

"Can the characters demonstrate how they feel by the way they move? Let's experiment."

SOME SPECIAL THOUGHTS ON USING PUPPETS:

☐ The puppeteer must always **move** the puppet when it speaks, so the audience will see the puppet **speaking**. If there are other puppets in the scene, only the ones who are speaking should be moving.

☐ Because the puppeteer is usually concealed from the audience, he must **speak up** and **project** his voice so the audience can hear what the puppet is saying.

☐ Children should have time to think about the personalities of their puppet so they can choose a voice that will best suit it.

☐ The puppeteer must keep the voice of the puppet consistent during the entire play.

☐ It helps if each puppet has a different sounding voice so the audience can tell which puppet is speaking.

☐ By using music, props and sound effects, the presentation can be made more interesting.

WARNING!

This book will not allow itself to sit idly on the shelf.
It will haunt you until it is USED!

These projects are rewarding, easy and successful.
The enthusiasm that results is too great to miss.

SO:

Get involved.

Explore.

Take a risk.

Shake hands with creativity.

Have fun!

Ron & Marsha

Paper Masks and Puppets was set in Optima type and printed by Magna Color Press, Inc., Seattle, Washington. The pages were Smyth bound and glued to the cover by Bayless Bindery, Seattle, to make this a permanent book.